chez moi

decorating your home and living like a Parisienne

SARAH LAVOINE

WITH DANIÈLE GERKENS

TRANSLATION FROM THE FRENCH BY WILLARD WOOD

ABRAMS IMAGE, NEW YORK

French Edition

Editor: Véronique Philipponnat

Designer: Delphine Delastre

Abrams Image Edition

Editor: Laura Dozier

Designer: Shawn Dahl, dahlimama inc

Production Manager: Denise LaCongo

Library of Congress Control Number: 2016936620

ISBN: 978-1-4197-2282-0

Printed and bound in China

10 9 8 7 6 5 4 3 2 1

ABRAMS The Art of Books
115 West 18th Street, New York, NY 10011
www.abramsbooks.com

CONTENTS

Me to You

DESIRE has always been my driving force, and wanting to awaken that same desire in the hearts of others is my passion. It comes from my education, from my parents, and also from my Polish roots. My father was director of *Vogue*, my mother an interior decorator. They doted on me, raised me to love my neighbor, to respect myself. They taught me to see the beauty of the world. At their side, I had the great privilege of learning to look at paintings, photographs, furniture, landscapes.

In the whirlwind of life, travel, and new experiences, I realized early on the value of having a cocoon, a home base, a safe harbor. I moved in, moved out, changed countries and neighborhoods, and always carried packed in my boxes the conviction that CREATING A SPACE FOR YOURSELF, appropriating your own world, is vital, no matter what the circumstances.

Yes, in the marathon race to happiness, one's environment plays a key role! A house is an overcoat, a freshly made bed we have the pleasure of rolling around in.

A HOME IS A SANCTUARY, a haven of peace, where we can let down our guard amid the mad race of our hectic lives.

Like you, I have to reconcile my family life and my professional life, organize my own life and my children's, be there for the man I love, and not neglect my friends. Like you, I juggle all these responsibilities, and like you, I do my best. Like you, I sometimes feel it's not enough. But I know that the sound of the key in the door, the subdued welcome of an entryway, the design of a living room, the charming simplicity of a child's bedroom, the light in a bathroom, the smell of a kitchen can soothe and comfort when the world outside is full of noise.

Grappling with space was an obvious thing for me to do. Turning things, turning them again, changing the lines, the furniture, and distilling this happiness for others is a great joy. My profession is an extension of my deep belief: BEING HAPPY IS ONE OF THE ARTS OF LIVING.

This is why I've decided to share my experience with you and to try and convince you, through my preferences, my ideas, my tricks—and not, I hope, without humor—that you deserve the best: first of all, at home!

The principle is simple: Your current living space is not an inevitable fate. The truth is that by moving two or three pieces of furniture EVERYTHING CAN CHANGE in a house, and in your life as well. A color, a floor, a lighting scheme, even a simple steamer trunk can improve your experience of daily life.

Travels aside, I have lived in Paris for most of my life, and many of the people who know me best have called me a true Parisienne. My advice in the pages to follow is imbued with this particular urban lifestyle and informed by the countless sources of inspiration that can be discovered in this vibrant city. I've included many of my recommended addresses, which are primarily intended to guide residents and visitors to Paris. But for those far away from the City of Light, the good news is that many of my favorite businesses operate worldwide, ship worldwide, or at the very least offer websites with images for inspiration. SO, WHILE MY APPROACH TO INTERIOR DESIGN AND TO LIFE IN GENERAL IS VERY MUCH ROOTED IN PARIS, IT CAN BE ADOPTED NO MATTER WHERE YOU LIVE.

Simplifying, putting things away, rearranging, stripping down, simply in order to breathe—that's the heart of my project. Come with me; we'll go together. And don't forget that if beauty pleases the eye, gentleness charms the soul.

Happy inner travels,

THE
Living Room

The living room is the heart of the house!
Children, friends, everyone has to feel at home
there: a comfortable couch, a soft rug, flattering
light . . . and the world is yours to do over.

To me, the living room is a marriage of materials and colors.

An element of modern design.

A light fixture is always a good way to introduce a vintage element.

Mix wood and marble for a dialogue between hot and cold materials.

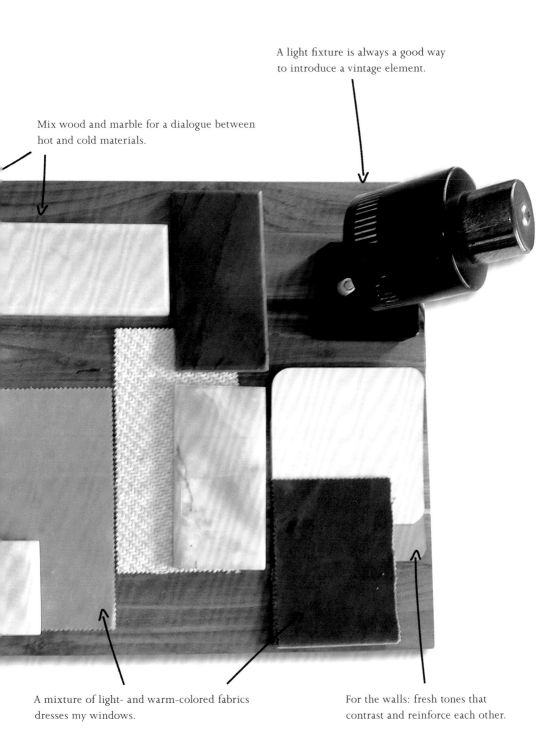

A mixture of light- and warm-colored fabrics dresses my windows.

For the walls: fresh tones that contrast and reinforce each other.

13

MY ESSENTIALS

A well-balanced living room is a subtle interplay between the furniture, comfortable accessories, colors, and materials.

THE COFFEE TABLE

You can't have a living room without a coffee table. I like vintage tables, organic-looking and made of raw wood, and set off with pretty 1950s ceramics. My advice? Don't hold back: Put several low tables around your living room and use some as a place to group books and objects.

MIRRORS

Fabulous allies for light and ambience! I like to cluster several on a single wall, playing with different shapes, sizes, and frame styles. I often put a big one over the mantelpiece, even if it's not a "classic" mirror. And I like to put them on either side of a dormer window to reflect the view and the light.

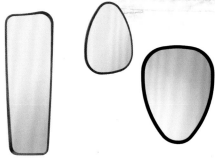

SOFAS

I like them big, wide, soft, and, if possible, in sets of two, arranged face-to-face, for conversations that go on all night.

CUSHIONS

Change cushions with the seasons (linen and cotton in summer, wool and sheepskin in winter). It lets you change your décor on a small budget. I always throw together a bunch of cushions of varied shapes, sizes, and designs.

THE RUG

It demarcates a central area in the living room, making an island for the sofas and tables. Choose a rug that is all one color, or an ethnic rug, or a striped one. You can also mix them together!

CURTAINS

To protect your privacy, to filter strong light, to define spaces and volumes . . .

LAMPS

Their light, whether diffused or direct, gives substance to the room. I like to have many light sources, and often mix styles—vintage, contemporary, and designer. And I distribute throughout the room as many floor lamps, swing-arm lamps, and low lamps as possible. These can be turned on or off according to the circumstances and your mood.

TIDYING UP IN
TEN MINUTES FLAT

Picking up the children's toys, sorting the magazines, tossing the stuff
that collects in piles: I hate spending too much time on it. So from the
beginning, I make sure to have plenty of storage places, like boxes, shelves,
and drawers. Any Legos left lying around, any stacks of books, any useless
objects—bingo! Back in their corner!

USE EVERY NOOK AND CRANNY

The space under a staircase, the corner of a room, the top of a wardrobe, the bottom of an angled wall—a house is full of small, underused spaces. Before deciding what to put where, list and measure everything.

INSTALL DRAWERS

Drawers on rollers are practical and easy to install under shelves, bookcases, or the couch. They provide extra storage space that disappears into the background.

ADD STEAMER TRUNKS

They're ideal for bulky items (cushions, blankets, children's toys). Put a seat cushion and some colored throw pillows on top and you've got a stylish mini-sofa!

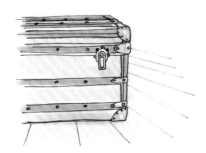

GO OVERBOARD ON BOXES

A good way to create visual order: Add boxes made of wood (light or dark), bamboo, woven fibers, cardboard— even reuse shoeboxes from a fancy store. Line up three of the same ones on a shelf or under a piece of furniture, and they look great!

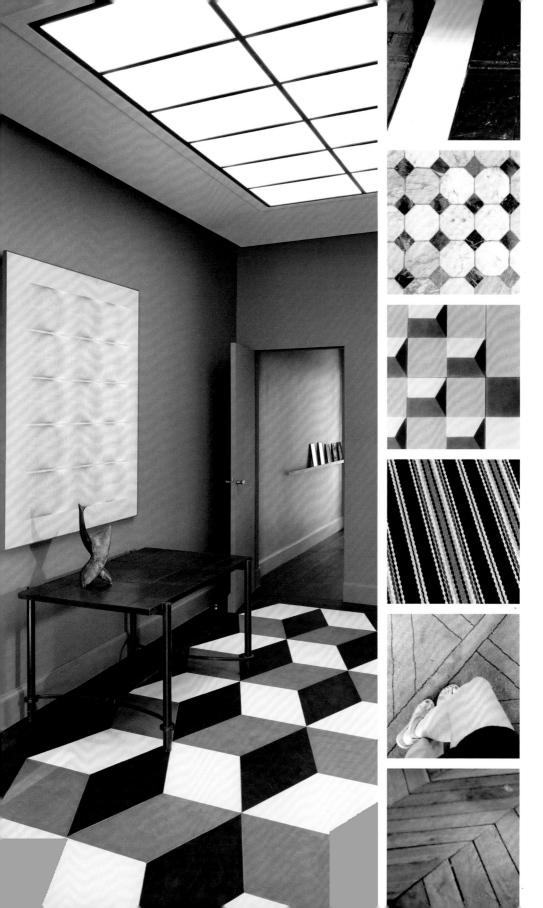

THE ART OF FLOORING

I pay great attention to the floor. I like everything: natural materials, woven fibers, parquet flooring, as well as carpets, rugs, cement tiles, concrete....

PARQUET FLOORING

What's better than a handsome parquet? The ideal: natural parquet with a simple pattern, sanded and waxed.

Another idea: Is your parquet a little worn? Instead of replacing it with new, soulless parquet, paint it with a good, durable floor paint, either in a single color (such as black, dark red, or navy blue) or in bands of contrasting colors (like black, dark plum, and white; or black and blue; or black and red).

RUGS

A rug warms up a room while also giving definition to the space. Rugs are very useful in the living room, marking a symbolic boundary around the sofas and chairs, making "rooms" within the room. This is true even if you have a tiny space. Try it, you'll see!

Another idea: Forget classic Oriental rugs, which can weigh down a decorative scheme. Instead, choose one from Morocco, or a color-field rug, or a Cogolin rug. Use them alone or in combinations, one next to another, for a cumulative effect.

TILES

I have used cement tiles in living rooms: It lets you play with neoclassical motifs but in a contemporary medium, and the tiles develop a nice patina over time. Lay down a color-field of tiles, accenting it with a single-color outline.

Another idea: Make a "rug" of tiles, laying them within a parquet floor to define a smaller space, particularly within a large living area.

CARPETING

Widely disparaged, carpeting has its benefits. When deep and of good quality, it affords comfort, coziness. I don't generally advise putting it in a living room, but it can be a sensible choice if the space is noisy or your rug budget is constrained.

Another idea: A more sophisticated but still inexpensive approach is to have the carpet trimmed to the contours of the room, leaving a space of eight inches (20 cm) along the walls.

GIVE YOURSELF LIGHT!

Lighting is crucial! It sets the tone and spirit of a place, creates density (depending on its color), sculpts space—and makes us look attractive. It requires an investment not necessarily of money, but of time, to find modern and vintage lamps to mix and match at Ikea, on eBay, or at your local flea markets.

CEILING LIGHTS

These days we tend to go out and find retro ceiling fixtures. A real one made of crystal to hang over the dining room table. Or a fake one in a vintage style to hang somewhat low, or grouped with others in a cluster. Hanging two or three together becomes a work of art! Above tables, drop them down fairly low for an intimate ambience.

INDIRECT LIGHT

Forget about spotlights in the living room. Nothing breaks the atmosphere the way lighting from the ceiling does. Use spots in a hallway, a bathroom, or the kitchen. What we want here is indirect lighting, using lamps of different heights and intensities—floor lamps, reading lamps, desk lamps—that can be moved if necessary.

YELLOW OR WHITE, CHOOSE YOUR LIGHT

It's crazy, there are a gazillion lightbulbs to choose from! Warm white (2,500 to 3,000 kelvins), bright white (3,500 to 4,100 kelvins), and daylight (5,000 to 6,500 kelvins). For me, it's no contest: warm white only, which gives a soft light similar to candles.

When light is art

Should we worship vintage?

When I get the blues, I know what
to do: I visit vintage websites and
buy myself some nice light fixtures.
For my birthday, I have been known
to buy myself a handsome vintage
lamp! I like lights by Italian designers.
Find a copy of *The Complete Designers'
Lights (1950–1990)*, edited by Clémence
and Didier Krzentowski, the founders
of a contemporary design gallery in
Paris. It's full of ideas.

CANDLE OBSESSION

I put them everywhere.

I go totally overboard: at home, at the office, in the country, in every room of the house, on tables, shelves, the mantel. Scented or unscented, XXL or tealight—I never have enough!

SCENTED CANDLES

Scent is a presence, almost a romantic presence. It instantly calls to mind memories, emotions. Lighting a candle is one of the first things I do in the morning, even at the office! My favorite scents? Fig, white flowers, wood fires in the winter, incense… Another option is a Diptyque scent diffuser, which looks like a work of art.

My advice

* Always buy candles made of natural wax, and ideally having a natural wick too. Synthetic candles can produce harmful vapors.

* Opt for high-quality candles that burn slowly and without smoke.

* Don't let a candle burn for longer than two or three hours at a time.

* Straighten the wick and recenter it regularly, once the wax has cooled off.

* Trim the wick often with scissors to keep the candle from smoking.

* Choose light, subtle scents so as not to make the atmosphere heavy.

* Try "flameless candles" that use LED lights, but choose ones made of wax, which give off a wonderful light.

* Group three or four candles together for greater effect, especially in a fireplace.

* Choose glass candlesticks to avoid the risk of fire, or use vases, glass bowls, lanterns. . . .

WHERE TO BUY CANDLES

* **Sarah Lavoine:** My preference obviously is for my own candles. The latest are inspired by my favorite poems. I've always paid attention to my products' quality and quiet harmony.
For sale at Sarah Lavoine boutiques:

9 rue Saint-Roch,
75001 Paris;
tel. +33 01 42 96 34 35

28 rue du Bac,
75007 Paris;
tel. +33 01 42 86 00 35

Find retailers at
www.sarahlavoine.com/en/

* **CFOC (Compagnie Française de l'Orient et de la Chine):** The candles are of good quality, and the scents are subtle. Some are in pretty glass pots that can be reused as vases or pencil jars.
170 boulevard Haussmann, 75007 Paris;
tel. +33 01 53 53 40 80

10 boulevard Raspail, 75007 Paris;
tel. +33 01 42 79 13 15

www.cfoc.fr

* **Diptyque:** An important brand, it has deservedly become a classic, as have its Figuier (Fig Tree) and Cyprès (Cypress) scents. A sure bet.
8 rue des Francs-Bourgeois, 75003 Paris;
tel. +33 01 48 04 95 57

34 boulevard Saint-Germain, 75005 Paris;
tel. +33 01 43 26 77 44

These are widely available in Europe and the US. Find retail locations and shop online at www.diptyqueparis.com

* **Astier de Villatte:** This brand also makes natural candles that come in attractive glass or porcelain containers and have light scents that suggest exotic places.
173 rue Saint-Honoré, 75001 Paris;
tel. +33 01 42 60 74 13

Find retailers at www.astierdevillatte.com

* **Diana Vreeland:** An exclusive line of candles. The best part? The candleholder, designed by Fabien Baron, made of smoked, faceted glass, which looks like a work of art.
Available at Colette, 213 rue Saint-Honoré, 75001 Paris; tel. +33 01 55 35 33 97
en.colette.fr

Find retailers at www.dianavreeland.com/beauty

* **Berluti:** The height of luxury. A collaboration between Cire Trudon and Berluti, these candles offer a rather masculine wood-and-leather scent and come in hand-cut crystal holders. An exceptional item.
31 rue Marbeuf, 75008 Paris;
tel. +33 01 53 53 11 00

9 rue du Faubourg-Saint-Honoré, 75008 Paris;
tel. +33 01 58 18 57 86

Find retail locations at www.berluti.com/en

USE BOLD COLORS

Despite what people think, colors don't make a room dark. They provide structure, as long as they're well chosen and well applied.

UNPOPULAR WITH DECORATORS

You always hear that white, pale gray, and cream-colored walls make a room look bigger and that they are colors you never tire of. So interior decorators neglect the more intense colors. This is a mistake. In the right amount, flashy colors can give a room character at no great expense. You don't need to move the walls, or invest in expensive furniture or works of art. All you need is a few cans of paint and some brushes and rollers, and you can change everything.

BLACK, THE DECORATORS' DARK HORSE

Black is a color that is often ignored. Yet black can provide warmth, set something off, or provide a wonderful backdrop for artworks, pictures, a view.... I use black to cover a wall, or put bands of black around a wall to form a frame, and sometimes around a window opening. I also like using black to transform parquet flooring.

WHITE IS NOW!

White is purity. And it's all the more luminous when set off against black or some other strong color, just the way lipstick sets off your skin color.

BLACK + WHITE + YELLOW

A magic trio that gives energy to a room! Especially when you choose a very saturated, sunny, warm yellow. Before actually applying paint to the walls, I always advise making a sketch using crayons on paper. Then paint the chosen colors onto 8.5 × 11-inch (30 × 20 cm) sheets of paper. Tack them to the walls and consider the effect before committing yourself. And never forget, it's only paint!

FOR EVERY ROOM, ITS OWN COLOR!

I like the idea of giving each room in the house a strong identity and a specific color. Blue I find particularly pleasing, because it strikes me as urbane, contemporary, and at the same time very restful and poetic, especially when set off by black. An important thing to know about color: The edges and finish need careful attention. If the effect is anything less than crisp, it can look like a mess.

I dream up color combinations that play off and enrich each other.

A light pink, used as an accent color, brings freshness to deep emerald.

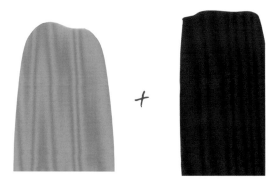

Contrast dark plum with vibrant pink.

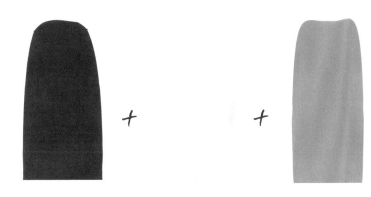

A trio of colors that, while cool in tone, is ever so soothing.

"Sarah blue" is a deep color that adapts to its environment. Veering at times toward turquoise, at others toward green, this shade comes alive according to the light and colors that surround it.

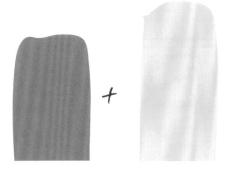

Make a large area of beige and structure it with a coppery green.

THE THING ABOUT WALLPAPER

I approve of wallpaper within limits.

The more contemporary choice is to use it as an element of decoration, on one wall or a section of a wall. Choosing the wrong paper or using too much of it can make things go seriously wrong!

My advice

* With wallpaper, less is definitely more. You adore it? Then go ahead, but carefully!

* Use wallpaper as a backdrop to theatricalize the wall behind the sofa, for instance, or a section of a wall, or a recessed area, or the surface behind shelves.

* Use textured wallpaper to suggest materials that might otherwise be costly, like brick, tile, or leather. Nowadays, you can find a startling range of easy-to-apply wallpapers that mimic various wall treatments.

* If you're not sure you'll like it, stay away from it. In interior design, having questions about something often means you already have your answer.

SOURCES FOR WALLPAPER

* **Nobilis:** An excellent company that has wonderful examples of trompe l'oeil wood (Cork III, Oak, Cypress).
29 rue Bonaparte, 75006 Paris;
tel. +33 01 43 29 21 50

Find retailers at www.nobilis.fr/?___store=cat_en

* **Élitis:** They carry paper that cost-effectively mimics a variety of wall treatments.
35 rue de Bellechasse, 75007 Paris;
tel. +33 01 45 51 51 00

Find retailers at www.elitis.fr/en

* **Bien Fait Paris:** Cécile Figuette, formerly a designer for Minakani Lab, opened this store to showcase her wallpapers and decorations, which can be shipped worldwide.
23 rue Saint-Paul, 75004 Paris

Shop online at www.bien-fait-paris.com/en

* **Au fil des Couleurs:** Provides an excellent selection of wallpapers in a variety of styles, including those by Mues Design.
31 rue de l'Abbé-Grégoire, 75006 Paris;
tel. +33 01 45 44 74 00

www.aufildescouleurs.com

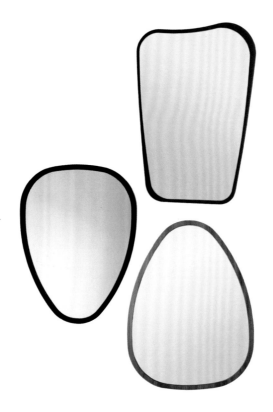

MOUNT EVERYTHING ON THE WALL!

Paintings, photographs, drawings, posters, Polaroids, mirrors, found objects... I hang up anything I possibly can—and always have! Sometimes I pack the items closely together, leaving hardly any free space. Sometimes I make a loose arrangement, with just one fine piece. Our walls say a lot about us.

THE PETERSBURG STYLE

What if we followed the example of one of the
most famous museums in the world? In Saint
Petersburg's State Hermitage Museum, artworks
invade even the smallest spaces on the walls. This
fashion had its hour of glory during the eighteenth
century, in the drawing rooms of the European
aristocracy. At the time, hanging paintings across
the entire surface of a wall was a common practice
in both Paris and London. Quantity and quality
went together, expressing both the richness and
the eclecticism of a person's tastes. This style can
be adapted to our lives today!

My tips on mixing and matching

* Use forceful lines: It's OK to make arrangements that look organic and a bit free-form, but not just any old way. The trick is to anchor them on a line that provides structure. Examples: Align several works along the same horizontal line, play with a diagonal, group pieces into a round or oval shape, cover a section of wall from floor to ceiling, or keep objects above the level of the door frames.

* Use one style of frame: To unify a set of works of varying colors, shapes, techniques, and materials, I like to use simple, identical frames of light oak with white mats, or a narrow black frame with a cream-colored mat. I also like floater frames.

* Add rhythm to your arrangements: Depending on the width of the mat, one or several images can be slid under a single piece of glass. It energizes a composition and breaks the monotony.

* Use all kinds of objects: A child's drawing, prettily framed, can hold its own against a work of primitive art. Tissue paper wrapping from an orange can be lovely. A set of postcards from a distant part of the world can enliven a section of wall. Beauty is everywhere!

* Make a plan: Children's drawings, art photos, postcards—anything is fair game, but it all comes down to balancing the colors. Before hanging an arrangement on the wall, lay it out on the floor until you get a balanced composition.

* The art of framing: From specialty frame shops to Internet sites to a retail store's ready-made frames, there are solutions to be found in every price range. Explore your local shops or try:

WhiteWall: A really phenomenal website that allows you to make professional prints of your own photos and have them framed. It's perfect if you're as overwhelmed as I often am!

us.whitewall.com

DON'T FORGET...

Consideration for others is the essence of good manners! The rules of etiquette have been relaxed in recent years, but using them can still warm one's relationships with others, making those connections closer and truer! And manners seem even more important when you are inviting people into your home or visiting someone else's.

ATTENTIVE GESTURES

They strengthen everyday relationships between friends, intimates, and children.... Being thoughtful is a form of politeness toward yourself and those around you. It often takes only a few seconds, or a few minutes: posting a Snapchat photo, sending a text message, making a quick call, sharing a FaceTime session—I try to pay as much attention as possible to those I love, even though there are only twenty-four hours in the day!

GIFTS

It doesn't take a costly gift to please someone. In fact, it's embarrassing to receive an overly expensive present, and to give one as well. When I'm invited to go somewhere, I keep things simple. I like to give a scented candle to a woman, and a bottle of good wine to a man—or the reverse!

LISTENING

I'm not very chatty. People tell me I listen a lot more than I talk. It's true. I don't like to talk about myself. Who wants to hear someone else get on her soapbox? Baroness Staffe, a nineteenth-century guru of the social graces, said: "One should mention oneself as little as possible; the subject is almost always bothersome or uninteresting to others." To listen is to observe, and to observe is to understand. When I listen, I get a better picture of what a person is telling or not telling me. This doesn't stop me from being open with my friends, of course, but I don't prattle on about "me me me" for hours on end.

ELEGANCE

There is no set recipe. Being natural is part of it. As are optimism, discretion, and understatement. Elegance is passing through life without jolting others, without upsetting them. It's being aware of other people's feelings. It's not complaining. And smiling, always smiling, but for real!

FLOWERS

Traditionally, you always thanked a hostess for a dinner by having flowers delivered the next day. Showing up carrying a bouquet was the height of bad manners. Today, the latter practice has gained popularity. But receiving a tidal wave of flowers at the last minute can be a problem as you're trying to greet your guests and whip together the veal ragout. My solution? I have a bouquet in a vase delivered to the hostess during the late afternoon before a dinner.

INVITATION

Forget the engraved card of yesteryear—that's unthinkable for a dinner invitation today! Our social codes are more relaxed. I often have guests over on weekday nights, but especially on weekends in the country. The house is open, friends drop by, things are informal. But everyone knows that it makes sense to call ahead to make sure there's room. And when I send out invitations, it's via WhatsApp, delivered to a whole group so everyone can agree on a date!

TABLE

I always try to set a pretty table. It takes hardly any extra time to lay out two glasses (one for wine, one for water), fold the napkins, and line up the silver properly, with those farthest from the plate for the first course. I also put a spoon and fork out for dessert, and to save time I stack the cheese and dessert plates on the kitchen counter beforehand!

WORDS

I like to hear proper speech at the table! We speak not of "eating," but of "dining"; we don't sing out "Bon appétit" before a meal. Also, we don't slice our bread; we break it. We don't talk about Bordeaux or Burgundies, but about wines from Bordeaux or Burgundy. It may seem old-fashioned. And yet these rules of etiquette are the basis of our French culture.

"THANKS"

It's the most magical word in the world, closely followed by "please," "good morning," and "good-bye." Obvious? Yes, but aren't you always a little surprised after a dinner not to get a quick call or a text message? Even if I have a temperature of 102°F the next morning, I send my thanks. It seems as necessary as breathing!

TELEPHONE

I'm addicted to my cellphone. Hopelessly. Unconditionally. During the day, on the weekend, in a car, in bed, I send text messages all the time, sending photographs, words. . . . I try to control myself in meetings, or over dinner, but it's not always easy! The telephone is what keeps me permanently in touch with those I love. Where do I draw the line? The Apple Watch. Looking at your watch constantly to check for emails—that's going too far!

My useful addresses

SOFAS AND CHAIRS

Three indispensable suppliers:

* **Cassina:** A big name in Italian design, and perfect reissues.
236 boulevard Saint-Germain, 75007 Paris; tel. +33 01 42 84 92 92
Find retailers at www.cassina.com

* **Maison HAND:** The best interior design store in Lyon, offering a careful sampling of ethnic/contemporary objects savvily chosen by its owners.
11 bis rue Jarente, 69002 Lyon; tel. +33 04 78 37 05 92
www.maison-hand.com

* **Etat de Siege**
1 quai de Conti, 75006 Paris; tel. +33 01 43 29 31 60
www.etatdesiege.com

DESIGN AND VINTAGE FURNITURE

* **Galerie Kreo:**
Basics, tables, storage solutions—phenomenal!
31 rue Dauphine, 75006 Paris; tel. +33 01 53 10 23 00

For the London location see www.galeriekreo.com/en

* **Chahan Gallery:** Showplace for a little-known designer specializing in American furniture of the 1950s and 1960s.
11 rue de Lille, 75007 Paris; tel. +33 01 47 03 47 00
www.chahan.com

* **Galerie MCDE:** Primary licensers for Pierre Chareau, the great early twentieth-century architect and designer who designed the celebrated Maison de Verre. A source for lamps and furniture.
1 rue Saint-Benoît, 75006 Paris; tel. +33 01 47 03 97 35
www.pierrechareau-edition.com

* **Galerie May:** Charles Tassin, an interior designer, and Maylis Queyrat, a contemporary artist, exhibit their creations.
23 rue de Lille, 75007 Paris; tel. +33 01 42 61 41 40
www.galerie-may.fr/pages/home/language:eng

* **Florence Lopez Antiquaire:** A specialist in twentieth-century antiques who displays her finds in a setting that is regularly reinvented.
18 rue du Dragon, 75006 Paris; tel. +33 01 40 49 08 12
www.florencelopez.com/en

* **Carpenters Workshop Gallery:** A gallery full of curiosities that is well worth the detour!
54 rue de la Verrerie, 75004 Paris; tel. +33 01 42 78 80 92
www.carpentersworkshopgallery.com

* **Galerie Hervouet**
40 rue de l'Université, 75007 Paris; tel. +33 01 42 61 24 18
www.galeriehervouet.fr

* **Marché aux Puces de Saint-Ouen:** The flea market in the town of Saint-Ouen.
142 rue des Rosiers, 93400 Saint-Ouen
www.marcheauxpuces-saintouen.com/1.aspx

* **James:** Interior design gallery with changing exhibits.
18-20 rue de Thorigny, 75007 Paris; tel. +33 01 40 09 97 41
www.james-paris.com

* **Maison Nordik**
159 rue Marcadet, 75018 Paris; tel. +33 06 22 07 21 07
www.maisonnordik.com

RUGS

* **Atelier LZC:** Lovely, timeless pieces with quasi-ethnic motifs.
2 rue Marcelin-Berthelot, 93100 Montreuil; tel. +33 01 42 87 81 34
www.atelierlzc.com

* **Urban Outfitters:** A lifestyle brand offering attractive, low-cost rugs with geometric motifs.
In BHV Marais, 52 rue de Rivoli, 75004 Paris; tel. +33 09 77 40 14 00

Find retail locations and shop online at www.urbanoutfitters.com

* **La Manufacture Cogolin:** A manufacturer with exceptional expertise in weaving wool, cotton, and raffia.
30 rue des Saints-Pères, 75007 Paris; tel. +33 01 40 49 04 30
www.manufacturecogolin.com

* **Chevalier Édition:** A melding of upscale craftsmanship and contemporary design.
94 rue Charles-de-Gaulle, 92200 Neuilly-sur-Seine;
tel. +33 01 46 98 95 59
Find retail locations at www.chevalier-edition.com/en-us/collection.aspx

* **Le Manach:** An exceptional company that's been making fabrics and rugs since 1829.
27 rue du Mail, 75002 Paris;
tel. +33 01 44 77 35 22
www.lemanach.fr/en

* **Galerie Diurne:** A designer and seller of classic and contemporary rugs.
45 rue Jacob, 75006 Paris;
tel. +33 01 42 60 94 11
www.diurne.com/_v2

UPHOLSTERY/FABRIC

* **Pierre Frey**
27 rue du Mail, 75002 Paris;
tel. +33 01 44 77 35 22
Find retailers at www.pierrefrey.com

* **Dominique Kieffer**
6 rue de l'Abbaye, 75006 Paris;
tel. +33 01 43 54 27 77
Find retailers at
www.dominiquekieffer.com

* **Élitis**
35 rue de Bellechasse, 75007 Paris;
tel. +33 01 45 51 51 00
Find retailers at www.elitis.fr/en

* **Dedar Milano**
20 rue Bonaparte, 75006 Paris;
tel. +33 01 56 81 10 95
Find retailers at www.dedar.com/en

* **Tensira**
21 place des Vosges, 75003 Paris;
tel. +33 06 79 39 49 90
www.tensira.com

* **Habu Textiles:** Maker of traditional Japanese fabrics of exceptional beauty!
Shop online at www.habutextiles.com

PAINTS

* **Ressource:** A fabulous company for wall paints, with extensive and refined offerings. I chose them to distribute my own line of paints.
2–4 avenue du Maine, 75015 Paris;
tel. +33 01 42 22 58 80

62 rue de la Boétie, 75007 Paris;
tel. +33 01 45 61 38 05

Find retailers at www.ressource-peintures.com/eng

* **Little Greene**
21 rue Bonaparte, 75006 Paris;
tel. +33 01 42 73 60 81
Find retailers at www.littlegreene.com

* **Seigneurie**
189 rue de la Croix-Nivert, 75015 Paris; tel. +33 01 40 60 03 13

8 rue Emile-Reynaud, 75019 Paris;
tel. +33 01 41 57 20 75
www.seigneurie.com

LIGHT FIXTURES

* **Bazar d'Électricité:** A shop with a treasure trove of light fixtures!
34 boulevard Henri-IV, 75004 Paris;
tel. +33 01 48 87 83 35
www.bazarelec.com

* **Espace Lumière**
167 boulevard Haussmann, 75008 Paris; tel. +33 01 42 89 01 15
www.espace-lumiere.fr

* **Le BHV Marais**
52 rue de Rivoli, 75004 Paris;
tel. +33 09 77 40 14 00
www.bhv.fr/en

* **Voltex**
29 boulevard Raspail, 75007 Paris;
tel. +33 01 45 48 29 62
www.voltex.fr

* **Artemide**
52 avenue Daumesnil, 75012 Paris;
tel. +33 01 43 44 45 42

Find retailers and shop online at www.artemide.com

* **Flos**
15 rue de Bourgogne, 75007 Paris;
tel. +33 01 53 85 49 90

Find retailers and shop online at www.flos.com

HOME FURNISHINGS

* **Anthropologie**
At BHV Marais, 52 rue de Rivoli, 75004 Paris; tel. +33 09 77 40 14 00

Find retailers and shop online at www.anthropologie.com

ART AND PHOTOGRAPHS

* **A. galerie:** A gallery belonging to Arnaud Adida dedicated to contemporary art and photography.
4 rue Léonce-Reynaud, 75016 Paris; tel. +33 06 20 85 85 85
www.a-galerie.fr

* **Kamel Mennour:** One of the key spaces for contemporary art in Paris today.
47 rue Saint-André-des-Arts, 75006 Paris; tel. +33 01 56 24 0363
www.kamelmennour.com

* **Galerie Perrotin**
76 rue de Turenne, 75004 Paris; tel. +33 01 42 16 79 79
www.perrotin.com

* **Galerie Jérôme Pauchant**
61 rue Notre-Dame-de-Nazareth, 75007 Paris; tel. +33 01 83 56 56 49
www.jeromepauchant.com

* **Galerie Dutko**
11 rue Bonaparte, 75006 Paris; tel. +33 01 56 24 04 20
www.dutko.com/home/?lang=en

* **Objetology:** Specialists from Spain in twentieth-century light fixtures, furniture, and household objects.
www.objetology.eu/?lang=en

* **CFOC**
170 boulevard Haussmann, 75007 Paris; tel. +33 01 53 53 40 80

10 boulevard Raspail, 75007 Paris; tel. +33 01 42 79 13 15
www.cfoc.fr

* **MOna MArket**
4 rue Commines, 75003 Paris; tel. +33 01 42 78 80 04
www.monamarket.com

* **La Maison d'Edition at Le Bon Marché**
24 rue de Sèvres, 75007 Paris; tel. +33 01 44 39 80 00
www.lebonmarche.com/en.html

* **Merci**
111 boulevard Beaumarchais, 75003 Paris; tel. +33 01 42 77 00 33
Shop at www.merci-merci.com/en/

* **The Conran Shop**
117 rue du Bac, 75007 Paris; tel. +33 01 42 84 10 01
Find retailers and shop online at www.conranshop.co.uk

* **Sentou**
29 rue François-Miron, 75004 Paris
www.sentou.fr/en

* **Yield:** An American home-furnishings company based in Saint Augustine, Florida, that offers spare, minimalist objects.
Find retailers and shop online at www.yielddesign.co

AND ON THE INTERNET

* **Gentlemen Designers:** For their secondhand objects, from Scandinavian furniture to custom-tailored pieces.
www.gentlemen-designers.fr

* **City-Furniture:** An excellent Belgian site for vintage pieces.
www.city-furniture.be

* **Made in Design:** A big player in the world of interior decoration on the Internet, a place that has everything—or nearly.
www.madeindesign.com

* **Auction.fr:** For online purchase of auction items.
www.auction.fr/_en

* **Cambi Casa d'Aste:** An Italian auction house that sells a little of everything. www.cambiaste.com/uk/cambi-aste.asp

* **eBay:** What's left to say that we don't know already? Often the worst, sometimes the best... www.ebay.com

THE
Kitchen

Today, kitchens are beautiful; we no longer hide
them away. In fact, just the opposite: We breakfast
there, dine there, gather there, converse there. . . .
It's pretty much where everything happens!

In the kitchen, I favor natural elements and vibrant colors.

I use the tea bowls I designed to serve up nibbles or condiments.

I select colored plates; it gives vibrancy to my cooking!

I often use *zelliges*, a kind of Moroccan tile, on the walls of a kitchen. They stand up well to the wear and tear of daily life and lend an air of sophistication.

Plain black oak gives character
to a kitchen counter.

I love growing aromatic plants:
They decorate the kitchen
and allow me to easily flavor
my cooking.

I like a nice set of porcelain teacups
for receiving friends in style.

MY ESSENTIALS

I like the idea of having beautiful things
all around me. Even in the morning when
I drink my tea in the kitchen!

PHOTOGRAPHS, POSTERS

I love them! Whether high-end prints or well-framed posters, they add to the spirit of a living space.

ELEGANT PRODUCTS

Wine bottles, jars of sauces or spices, and olive oil bottles with pleasing graphic designs are perfect for making mini-collections, like in a luxury deli.

A MOOD-BOARD REFRIGERATOR

Snapshots, attractive postcards, images cut from magazines . . . I like using the fridge as a mood board, but the magnets should be discreet!

A MINI-LIBRARY

I have a collection of handsome cookbooks in my kitchen—as much for inspiration as for the look.

HANGING LIGHTS

They change everything! I like them in pairs and on the large side. If the ambience feels too unrelentingly urban, I'll disrupt it with a rattan hanging light.

A RUG

A bright kilim makes a kitchen cozier and keeps water spills from staining the floor. I just toss it in the washing machine on the "wool" setting from time to time.

HIDE WHATEVER'S UGLY

You don't need to spend a fortune to have a nice kitchen! It's more a question of a good concept and good choices.

For a kitchen to be beautiful, you have to give it the same attention that you give to other rooms. More even, because it's more complicated, with all those household appliances. The trick is to give the space unity by using the same sleek facing on all the surfaces. My favorites are natural oak, lacquered white, or black, which is always elegant, picked out at a kitchen specialist's or simply at Ikea.

The refrigerator

The dishwasher

I hide...

* **The rice cooker:** A great appliance, but it should live in the cupboard unless you use it every day. The look is too stodgy.

* **The food processor:** Some cooks use it constantly. Not me. I prefer to keep it off the counter.

* **The steam cooker:** A little gadgety, no? If you're a fan of steam cooking, why not get a steam oven? Otherwise, you can achieve the same effect with a colander, a pot, and a lid.

A trick

Hang pots, pans, utensils, and all kinds of
kitchen tools on a wall to save space on
the counter and in cabinets.

WHERE DO YOU PUT THEM?

So as not to disrupt the kitchen's harmony,
I group appliances together in a corner,
making sure at the outset that there will be
enough electric sockets. Can't have electrical
cords lying around!

INVEST IN GOOD-LOOKING APPLIANCES

The refrigerator, stove, oven . . . you look
at them and use them every day. It's worth
making a little extra investment and opting
for the stainless-steel model, which is more
elegant. Then you can leave them in plain
sight. Hide the other appliances (dishwasher,
washing machine, clothes dryer) behind a
surface that matches the rest of the kitchen.
There, done! The exception would be a brightly
colored Smeg refrigerator, which looks like a
work of art.

STAY ON TOP OF THE CLUTTER

Rather than hide what's ugly, you can avoid
ugliness to begin with. Even the most beautiful
kitchen in the world will start looking terrible
if it's messy. I put cleaning products in the
cupboards, I forbid the children to leave their
stuff lying around, I wipe the counters clean.
What's left? A pretty collection of bottles, a few
spices, a handsome coffeemaker . . .

COME FOR DINNER

I love having people over! The fact is, there are always people
around the house, both in Paris and in the country. And all the
guests gather at the table for lunch or dinner.

Entertaining in the country

SETTING THE TABLE

* A pretty tablecloth of colored linen

* Linen napkins, not matching

* Crystal glasses for wine and water

* White and/or colored plates, not necessarily matching, but always hewing to a color theme

* Silver or silver-plated cutlery

* Flowers set out in little glasses

CHOOSING THE MENU

I often make pasta or a risotto. Another option is a fish carpaccio, because I'm crazy about sashimi! And everyone has to pitch in to help with the preparations.

All recipes serve 4 to 6 people.

FISH CARPACCIO

A fresh, quickly prepared first course

Get your fishmonger to thinly slice 3½ pounds (1.5 kg) of fish (seabream, salmon, sea bass). Lay the slices out on large platters and cover them with plastic wrap. Serve them with a soy vinaigrette (soy sauce + sesame oil + rice vinegar + grated ginger) or an herb sauce (grated ginger + chopped scallions + minced garlic + slivered shallots cooked for 1 minute in oil).

TRUFFLE PASTA

Perhaps my favorite food . . .

A day or two ahead, grate 1–2 ounces (30–50 g) of black truffle into 1 pint (500 g) of heavy cream. Cover and refrigerate. Cook 1 box of spaghetti in a big pot of water, draining the pasta 3 minutes before it's al dente. Meanwhile, warm the cream over low heat in a large sauté pan. Add 1 tablespoon of the cooking water and the spaghetti. Cook it gently for 2–3 minutes, stirring with a wooden spoon. Add salt and pepper, serve the pasta on hot plates, and grate fresh truffle over it.

RISOTTO

A basic dish that's highly adaptable

In a Dutch oven, sauté a large chopped onion in 6 tablespoons (90 ml) of olive oil. After 3 minutes, add 4 cups of arborio rice. Continue to sauté until the rice turns translucent. Moisten with 1½ cups (400 ml) of dry white wine. Then add 3 quarts (3 L) of chicken broth, a ladleful at a time, stirring regularly, and cook it for about 20 minutes over a low flame. Complete the risotto by taking it off the stove and stirring in 7 ounces (200 g) of grated Parmesan and 7 ounces (200 g) of butter.

Ideas for risotto:

✻ Grate a truffle over the risotto as you serve it.

✻ Just before removing the risotto from the stove, add peas, thinly sliced zucchini lightly sautéed in olive oil so that it still has some crunch, and baby spinach.

✻ Add diced pumpkin sautéed in olive oil and some diced blue cheese (Roquefort, gorgonzola).

✻ Add porcini mushrooms sautéed in olive oil and parsley pesto (garlic + parsley + roasted hazelnuts + salt + pepper + olive oil).

PAVLOVA

A spectacular and easy-to-make dessert

Whip 6 egg whites. When they're almost firm, add 1¾ cups (350 g) of sugar in several batches. Beat until the mixture is firm and glossy, then add, while still beating, 1 tablespoon of cornstarch. Drop disks of egg white onto a baking sheet lined with parchment paper. Cook for 1½–1¾ hours in an oven preheated to 250°F (120°C). Turn off the oven and leave the meringues inside to dry with the oven door ajar. Whip 3½ cups (800 ml) of cold heavy cream with the scraped seeds of 2 split vanilla pods and ½ cup (100 g) of sugar. Dollop the whipped cream onto the meringues. Top with red fruit.

Entertaining in Paris

CÔTE DE BOEUF

Preheat the oven to 450°F (240°C) for at least
15 minutes. Season rib steak with salt and pepper. In
a frying pan, brown the rib steak on both sides for
1–2 minutes. Place the meat on a baking sheet and bake
it for 25 minutes (for a 3½-pound [1.5 kg] steak). Remove
the steak, cover it in foil, and wait 5 minutes before
carving it. Serve it with herb butter (salted butter +
minced garlic + chopped parsley, mint, chervil, and basil).

POTATOES EMMANUELLE

Peel 2–2½ pounds (1 kg) of potatoes and cut into
large cubes. Cook in 2 quarts (2 L) of chicken broth.
After 20 minutes, drain and transfer the potatoes to a
frying pan with 2 ounces (50 g) of butter and ⅓ cup
(100 ml) of olive oil. Add salt. Sauté over low heat
for 15–20 minutes, or until they are crisp. These are a
perfect accompaniment to a rib steak and a green salad.

CITRUS SALAD

A light, fresh dessert

Remove the peels of 2 oranges and 1 grapefruit and cut
the flesh into segments. In a salad bowl, mix the fruits,
1 tablespoon of cane syrup, 1 tablespoon of orange
flower water, the seeds of ½ pomegranate, and a few
sprigs of lemon balm. Refrigerate for about 2 hours.
To serve, spoon the salad into wine glasses, pour ⅓ cup
(100 ml) of chilled champagne into each glass, and
serve immediately.

A BRUNCH WITH FRIENDS

Summer and winter, I always have friends who stop by for Sunday
brunch. It makes for a crowded table, with the children at one end, adults
at the other, and laughter everywhere! These recipes are some of my
favorites and serve 4 to 6 people.

GUACAMOLE

A simple recipe that everyone loves!
Mix 2 ripe avocados with the juice of 1 lime, a chopped
and seeded tomato, a small handful of cilantro leaves, salt,
pepper, a little Tabasco, and a thinly sliced scallion. Serve
with toasted rounds of baguette.

WHITE PIZZA

Created by my friend Michel for a pal of ours
who is allergic to tomatoes
Spread a layer of ricotta on rolled-out pizza dough. Add
slices of zucchini and mozzarella di bufala, and drizzle with
olive oil. Cook for 20 minutes in an oven preheated to 400°F
(210°C). Before serving, sprinkle with basil leaves and
roasted pine nuts.

TOMATO AND CHORIZO PIZZA

A pizza for grown-ups!
On rolled-out pizza dough, spread a layer of homemade
tomato sauce. Add cherry tomatoes, mozzarella di bufala,
slices of chorizo, basil, and olive oil. Cook for 20 minutes in
an oven preheated to 400°F (210°C).

GREEN BEAN, ASPARAGUS, SHRIMP, AND MANGO SALAD

A fresh, savory salad
Start with several large handfuls of mixed salad greens in
a salad bowl. Add ⅓ pound (150 g) of green beans, tipped
and tailed, blanched for 5 minutes in salted boiling water,
and cooled. Also add the tips of a bundle of asparagus
cooked for 4 minutes and cooled. Slice and add the flesh
of 2 mangoes. Skin and devein ¾ pound (400 g) of shrimp
and add them to the salad. Toss with a vinaigrette made
of ½ cup (100 ml) olive oil, 1 teaspoon of Dijon mustard,
1 teaspoon of honey, 1–2 drops of Tabasco, and 1 tablespoon
of cider vinegar. Add salt and pepper to taste.

FRUIT TART

Mix together 8 tablespoons (150 g) of room-temperature
unsalted butter, 1 cup (115 g) of confectioners' sugar,
½ teaspoon of vanilla sugar, a pinch of salt, and 1⅔ cup
(250 g) of flour. When the mixture has a sandy texture, add
an egg and work it into the dough gently. Refrigerate the
dough for at least 2 hours, then roll it out between two
sheets of parchment paper. Butter a tart pan and sprinkle it
with turbinado sugar. Line the pan with the dough. Slice the
fruit (you can use apples, pears, apricots, or even berries),
add them to the tart, and cook for 30 minutes in an oven
preheated to 350°F (180°C).

A BIRTHDAY PARTY

Having three children and numerous friends means that birthdays come around often! But I always try to make them magical moments. . . .

* Large helium balloons, paper plates, and cups to keep breakage down (Monoprix or Petit Pan: 39 and 76 rue François-Miron, 75004 Paris), and candies everywhere! I like them too. . . . My favorites? Those plump little Fraises Tagada and gummy bears.

* A 10-minute chocolate cake? Easy.

Put 7 ounces (200 g) of Valrhona dark chocolate in a glass bowl. Add 2 cups (500 ml) of very hot water. After 5 minutes, the chocolate will have melted and the water can be carefully poured off. Add 3 tablespoons of butter and melt in the microwave. Add ½ cup (100 g) of sugar, ¾ cup (75 g) of almond flour, ½ cup (75 g) of all-purpose flour, and ½ teaspoon of baking powder. Mix everything together. Pour into a microwave-safe baking dish and cook in the microwave for 4 minutes at full power. Sprinkle with confectioners' sugar before serving.

CHEF'S RECIPES

Thanks go to my favorite chefs, who made these recipes especially for me.

BASIL BEEF TARTARE BY AXEL MANES

* Chef at Atelier de Joël Robuchon
5 rue de Montalembert, 75007 Paris

Serves 4

Cut approximately 2 pounds (1 kg) of beef into small dice without mincing them. Put a deep serving dish in the freezer for 5–10 minutes. Use it to mix the meat with 2–3 ounces (75 g) of Parmesan finely cut with a knife; 1 bunch of basil, chopped; and the following, also chopped: 1–2 ounces (40 g) of gherkins, 2 small shallots, and 1 ounce (20 g) of small capers. Grind a generous quantity of pepper over the meat, add 1 fresh egg yolk, 1 tablespoon of mild mustard, ¾ cup (200 ml) of grapeseed oil, 2 tablespoons of extra virgin olive oil, 2 tablespoons of red wine vinegar, and 1 large pinch of fleur de sel. Serve with a well-seasoned mesclun salad and large, crispy french fries.

CALAMARI À LA CARBONARA BY JEAN-FRANÇOIS PIÈGE

* Chef at Jean-François Piège
7 rue d'Auguessau, 75008 Paris

Serves 4

Cut 7 ounces (200 g) of paprika-rubbed smoked thick-cut bacon into thin dice. Trim about 1 pound (400 g) of calamari into long, narrow strips about the width of spaghetti. Season with salt and olive oil, then grill for several minutes. In a small saucepan, reduce 1 cup (250 ml) of heavy cream, then add 3 ounces (80 g) of grated Parmesan and set aside. Pour the hot cream over the calamari and add 3 tablespoons of chopped chives. Mix well and grind pepper generously over it. Divide the calamari and serve in deep dishes. Divide and add the bacon to each plate. Before serving, add more pepper and a little grated Parmesan. Serve each dish with 1 raw egg yolk in a half egg shell, allowing your guests to stir to incorporate, as desired.

POTATOES PIERRE GAGNAIRE

* Chef at the restaurant Pierre Gagnaire
6 rue Balzac, 75008 Paris

Serves 6

Wash and dry 2 pounds (1 kg) of potatoes. Lay the potatoes on a thick layer of kosher salt in an ovenproof dish. Bake for 30 minutes at 400°F (200°C). Check for doneness with the tip of a knife. When they are cooked, halve the potatoes, remove the flesh, and pass it through a ricer or food mill without letting it cool. Add salt and pepper. Make 12 puck-like disks about 2 inches (5 cm) in diameter and slightly indented in the center. Roll them in bread crumbs. Chop and mix together 5 Medjool dates, 5 dried apricots, and 5 dried figs. Put some of this mixture on each of the disks, along with a knob of Brie de Meaux. Slip them into the oven for 2–3 minutes, just long enough to melt the cheese. Serve each person two of the disks, along with a scattering of mesclun.

MARINATED SALMON À LA THIERRY MARX

* Chef at the restaurant Sur Mesure par Thierry Marx
251 rue Saint-Honoré, 75001 Paris

Serves 4

Using a mortar and pestle, grind together ¼ cup (80 g) of salt, ¼ cup (80 g) of sugar, 1 tablespoon of coarse pepper, 10 sprigs of parsley, and ½ bunch of dill. The resulting paste should be fairly moist. Add 2 cups (500 ml) of dry white wine, then pour the mixture into a dish. Carefully wipe a 2-pound (1 kg) fillet of salmon with its skin still on with a paper towel. Place the fillet in the dish. Cover with plastic wrap and leave it to marinate for 24 hours in the refrigerator. Rinse the fish in cold water and wipe it dry. Put it in the freezer for 15–20 minutes. Measure out 1 cup (250 ml) of soy cream, add salt and pepper, then grate into it 1 ounce (25 g) of peeled horseradish. Put a little of this sauce on each plate, along with a drizzle of honey. Cut the fish into ½-inch (1 cm) thick slices without breaking the skin. Put the fish on the plates and serve with horseradish cut into long strips.

THE ART OF THE TABLE: THE ABCS

In France, we have very strict traditions about the right and wrong ways to set a table. I tend to allow a wide range of creativity, as long as the basics are observed. Of course, on a day-to-day basis, it's all right to keep things low-key.

DINNERWARE

What's the best way to choose plates and dishes? Follow your instinct, but don't forget that their role is to set off what you're going to eat.

CARAFES

I like to attend to every detail of a table, and I find that wine carafes immediately give it a bit of chic. Not to mention that decanting wine into a carafe helps it open up, become suppler.

NAPKINS

No paper! I find the feel of paper napkins quite unpleasant. I buy soft-washed linen napkins in natural colors, often with a pretty border.

NAPKIN RINGS

In the old days, the regulars at a bistro all had their own napkin rings. I love that! So for each of my friends, I commissioned a round wooden napkin ring, a very simple one with his or her name engraved on it.

CANDLEHOLDERS

Someone crazier about candles than I am is hard to imagine. If I could light my world entirely with candles, I would!

GLASSES

I'm a wine drinker, preferably red and from the Bordeaux region. I can't imagine anything prettier for serving it in than crystal glasses.

TABLECLOTHS

I belong to no particular camp, but I think they should be on the plain side. No big, wild motifs that are going to give the table a heavy look.

FLATWARE

Yes, silver can be splendid. Especially if it's old silver. But keeping it polished is a chore. To save time, I turn to sensible stainless-steel flatware for everyday use, or chopsticks.

My useful addresses

DINNERWARE

The choices in Paris are fantastic, but it is also nice to weave in international influences. From Morocco, I often bring back glazed green Berber pottery, including wonderful serving dishes, bowls, and a few plates. I'm also a fan of antique English crockery ferreted out in secondhand stores and used as mismatched serving pieces.

* **CFOC:** For its spectacular selection of fine porcelain.
170 boulevard Haussmann, 75008 Paris; tel. +33 01 53 53 40 80

10 boulevard Raspail, 75007 Paris; tel. +33 01 42 79 13 15

www.cfoc.fr

* **Hermès:** Luxury porcelain, with some magnificent designs. For mixing and matching.
24 rue du Faubourg Saint-Honoré, 75008 Paris; tel. +33 01 40 17 46 00

Find retailers and shop online at www.hermes.com

* **Bernardaud:** For porcelain that never goes out of fashion.
11 rue Royale, 75001 Paris; tel. +33 01 47 42 82 66

Find retail outlets at www.bernardaud.fr

* **Jars:** For its spare and very sturdy stoneware.
Find retail outlets at www.jarsceramistes.com/home

* **Sentou:** For dinnerware in the bold colors favored by Brigitte de Bazelaire.
29 rue François-Miron, 75004 Paris; tel. +33 01 42 78 50 60
www.sentou.fr/en

* **Ikea:** An obvious place to buy the basics, which can then be set off with more chic or rarer pieces bought elsewhere.
Find retail outlets and shop online at www.ikea.com

* **The Conran Shop:** A store that consistently offers a clever mix of designer pieces and utilitarian ones.
117 rue du Bac, 75007 Paris; tel. +33 01 42 84 10 01

Find retailers and shop online at www.conranshop.co.uk

* **Dibbern:** A German brand of porcelain that is very refined while at the same time modern.
Available at Printemps Haussmann, 64 boulevard Haussmann, 75009 Paris; tel. +33 01 42 82 50 00

Find retailers at www.dibbern.de/en/home.html

* **Beldine:** A fair-trade project in Marrakech, where the tableware is hand-painted by women.
Information can be found at www.facebook.com/Beldine.atelier/

* **House Doctor:** A Danish design brand offering spare, simple dishware.
Find retail outlets at en.housedoctor.dk

* **Broste Copenhaguen:** A Danish design brand that also creates very beautiful tableware.
Find retail outlets at www.brostecopenhagen.com

GLASSWARE AND CRYSTAL

* **Baccarat:** Because it's a historic company, its glassware is superb, and I've always known it. My favorite? The Harcourt, a classic.
11 place des Etats-Unis, 75116 Paris; tel. +33 01 40 22 11 22

Find retailers and shop online at us.baccarat.com

* **LSA International:** Its glasses are sturdy, nice, and inexpensive. I particularly like its designs in recycled glass, whose colors range from white to a very pale green.
Find retail outlets at www.lsa-international.com/stockists

* **Riedel:** For its excellent crystal wine glasses, which have a high quality-to-price ratio.
Find retail outlets at www.riedel.com/?slm=1

TABLE LINENS

At one time, I made my own by dyeing old sheets but now I purchase them from . . .

* **Merci:** For its linen table-cloths—colorful, poetic, sturdy.
111 boulevard Beaumarchais, 75003 Paris; tel. +33 01 42 77 00 33

Shop online at www.merci-merci.com/en

* **Chiarastella Cattana:** A carefully kept secret in Venice, for old-fashioned damask table-cloths, beautiful tea towels, napkins . . .
San Marco 3357 (San Samuele), 30124 Venice, Italy; tel. +39 041 522 43 69

Find retail outlets at www.chiarastellacattana.com/eng/chiarastella_cattana.html

APPLIANCES

* **Cuisine Viking:** Professional-quality products—especially its magnificent kitchen ranges—for demanding cooks.
Find retail outlets at www.cuisine-viking.com

* **La Cornue:** For some, this is the Rolls-Royce of stoves. In any case, these classic models never look out of place, whatever your decorating style.

54 rue de Bourgogne, 75007 Paris;
tel. +33 01 46 33 84 74

Find retail outlets at
www.lacornue.com/en

* **AGA:** A Swedish invention, these cast-iron ranges that hold heat are reputed to cook food without drying it out. I like them mostly for the amazing range of colors they come in.
11 rue du Bac, 75007 Paris;
tel. +33 01 42 61 19 01

Find retail outlets at
www.agamarvel.com/aga

* **Gaggenau:** Robust and efficient appliances, and so beautiful you want to give them a place of honor.
7 rue de Tilsitt, 75017 Paris;
tel. +33 01 58 05 20 20

Find retail outlets at
www.gaggenau.com/us

* **Smeg:** For a superb refrigerator, but also for ovens, cooktops, etc., with wonderfully sleek lines.
83 boulevard de Sébastopol, 75003 Paris; tel. +33 01 42 78 67 25

Find retail outlets at
www.smegusa.com

* **Magimix:** This French maker of countertop appliances is unrivaled for its food processors, toasters, electric kettles, etc. Their products are well made, handsome, and compact.
Available at department stores and specialty cookware outlets.
www.magimix.com/usa-canada

POTS AND PANS

Think quality, not quantity. You don't need a gigantic arsenal of pots and pans to cook. Two skillets, a few saucepans, and a Dutch oven and you're all set to work wonders.

* **KnIndustrie:** An Italian company, for its transparent saucepan, made of borosilicate, which looks like a work of art.

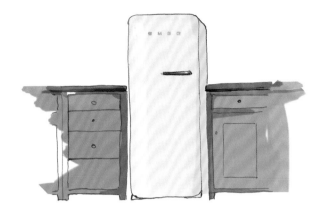

Available at Bon Marché,
24 rue de Sèvres, 7508 Paris;
tel. +33 01 44 39 80 00

Find retailers at www.knindustrie.it/en

* **Le Creuset:** For its oval Dutch ovens, timeless classics, in either traditional black cast-iron or colorful enamel. My advice? Ideally, own two of them, one about twelve inches (30 cm) wide, big enough for a chicken, and a larger one (sixteen inches [40 cm]) in which to cook a roast for eight people.
Find retailers at www.lecreuset.com

ARTISANAL FOODS
BUTCHERS

* **Hugo Desnoyer:** A star among butchers, he supplies even the Élysée Palace. Unfortunately, his shop is on the far side of the Seine from my house. The solution is to order meat from him through www.lehautdupanier.com.
45 rue Boulard, 75014 Paris;
tel. +33 01 45 40 76 67

28 rue du Docteur-Blanche, 75016 Paris; tel. +33 01 46 47 83 00

www.hugodesnoyer.fr

* **Archibald Gourmet:** For the carnivore who wants excellence in beef, it's all here: Angus, Wagyu.... Exceptional prime rib, the kind that makes the reputations of the best tables, is now available for home delivery.
www.archibaldgourmet.com

CHEESE

I love cheese. Especially when it's runny and smells strong. My favorites? Livarot, Saint Félicien, Pont l'Évêque, the Rocamadours, Appenzellers, sheep's milk tome ... Along with a glass of good wine, some bread, and a salad, it's enough to make me happy.

* **Fromagerie Quatrehomme:** Marie Quatrehomme was named a Meilleur Ouvrier de France (MOF) in 2000, and her skill at ripening is unequaled!
La Maison du Fromage, 62 rue de Sèvres, 75007 Paris;
tel. +33 01 47 34 33 45

La Fromagerie d'Issy-les-Moulineaux, 9 rue du Général-Leclerc, 92130 Issy-les-Moulineaux;
tel. +33 01 55 92 00 12

La Fromagerie du Rendez-Vous, 4 rue du Rendez-vous, 75012 Paris;
tel. +33 01 40 21 90 19

www.quatrehomme.fr/index_en.html

* **Fromagerie Barthélemy:** Another great name in the cheese world. Recently taken over by Nicole, this old-fashioned store brims with wonderful cheeses, including creamy Bries and earthy Saint Nectaires.
51 rue de Grenelle, 75007 Paris;
tel. +33 01 45 48 56 75
www.rolandbarthelemy.com

PATISSERIES AND SUCH

While I don't have much of a sweet tooth, I will cross the length of Paris for a good dessert. . . .

* **Les Petits Mitrons:** Their fruit tarts are unbelievable. Why? Because they powder their tart molds with sugar, which caramelizes on the dough.
26 rue Lepic, 75018 Paris; tel. +33 01 46 06 10 29

* **Aux Merveilleux de Fred:** One of its cakes, mixing crème Chantilly and meringue in a style from the north of France, quickly became legendary, and I'm crazy about it!
2 rue Monge, 75005 Paris; tel. +33 01 43 54 63 72
www.auxmerveilleux.com/home_en

* **Jacques Genin:** A self-taught god among the royalty of chocolate, Genin is particularly known for his fragrant ganaches and stupendous caramels (especially the passion fruit).
133 rue de Turenne, 75003 Paris; tel. +33 01 45 77 29 01
www.jacquesgenin.fr

FRUITS AND VEGETABLES

Like everyone, I'm always on the run. So I buy my produce at the market on weekends, or I order it on the Internet.

* **Marché Biologique Raspail:** One of the rare organic street markets in Paris.
Sunday mornings on boulevard Raspail between the rue du Cherche-Midi and the rue de Rennes, 75006 Paris

* **Marché Président-Wilson:** I go there for the vegetables of Joël Thiébault, the super-fresh fish, and the charcuterie.
Every Wednesday and Saturday, avenue du Président-Wilson, between rue Debrousse and place d'Iéna, 75016 Paris

GROCERY STORES

* **Workshop Issé:** For its selection of Japanese teas, rare vinegars, soy sauces . . .
11 rue Saint-Augustin, 75002 Paris; tel. +33 01 42 96 26 74
www.workshop-isse.fr

* **Épices Roellinger:** A magical place with an unbelievable selection of spices and a "vanilla cellar" where, when you take a breath, you set off on a trip.
51 bis rue Saint-Anne, 75002 Paris; tel. +33 01 42 60 46 88
www.epices-roellinger.com/?lang=en

* **La Grande Épicerie de Paris:** Often maligned, but seldom matched. It carries a wonderful mix of classic and super-edgy items, recent discoveries, and tried-and-true products, and its prepared foods are excellent.
38 rue de Sèvres, 75007 Paris; tel. +33 01 44 39 81 00
www.lagrandeepicerie.com/en.html

* **Izraël:** An Ali Baba's cave with bulging sacks of spices and exotic specialties. Its recommendations are always on target.
30 rue François Miron, 75004 Paris; tel. +33 01 42 72 66 23

* **Maison Plisson:** A brand-new "deluxe epicerie" with fresh produce, bread, pastries, and even a nice restaurant with a big terrace—great in the summertime.
93 boulevard Beaumarchais, 75003 Paris; tel. +33 01 71 18 19 09
www.lamaisonplisson.com

WINE STORES

Wine is serious business. I trust my suppliers.

* **Caves Augé:** There's no one better than Marc Sibard to point you toward a hard-to-find grand cru or a small label on its way up.

116 boulevard Haussmann, 75008 Paris; tel. +33 01 45 22 16 97
www.cavesauge.com

* **Eugen Grand Vin:** An excellent website that specializes in wines from Bordeaux. Great for buying newly released wines.
www.eugen-grandvin.com

TEA

I drink tiny amounts of coffee and vast amounts of tea, especially green and Japanese teas. My favorites: sencha, genmaicha with roasted rice, and white tea.

* **Jugetsudo:** The official suppliers to the court in Japan, they have opened a lovely store on the Left Bank offering teas of high quality.
95 rue de Seine, 75006 Paris; tel. +33 01 46 33 94 90
www.jugetsudo.fr/?___store=en&___from_store=fr

* **Mariage Frères:** This Paris-based company offers teas of proven value. Its flavored blends can be drunk hot or cold according to the season.
13 rue des Grands-Augustins, 75006 Paris; tel. +33 01 40 51 82 50

30 rue du Bourg-Tibourg, 75004 Paris; tel. +33 01 42 72 28 11

www.mariagefreres.com/UK/welcome.html

Entries, Halls, Attics, & Stairways

How to make the best use of your odd bits of space?
My motto is:
"No space is pointless; just find the right use for it."
A hallway or an entry can seem boring. But it doesn't
take much to make it useful and attractive!

THE ENTRY AND HALLS

The entry sets the tone for the house, and the hallways are its extension.
We don't normally think of accenting them, yet these long, narrow spaces
can be put to wonderful uses.

THINK DECORATION

I like to hang photographs all along the
hallways, either by mounting them in arrays
from floor to ceiling or by installing rimmed,
two-inch-deep shelves to display images on.

FURNISH THE ENTRYWAY

A crucial item for the entry is a console table.
There should be a container on it for small
change, keys, subway tickets—what we call
a *vide-poche*, a receptacle for what's in your
pockets when you come through the door.

CREATE ARRANGEMENTS

A wall of hats, rows of scarves ... Groupings
of objects can perk up an entryway.

GIVE IT COLOR

Because they are generally pass-through zones
with limited surface areas, they are ideal
for testing strong colors. Blue, black, red,
deep green—your chromatic range can be
extended here.

Another idea: Experiment with bands of
color on the walls. Example: red along the
bottom and white above, with a black line in
the middle (see pages 36–37 for some good
combinations).

EYES ON THE FLOOR

Handsomely patterned cement tiles, a sturdy
flat-weave rug (Hartley & Tissier), a bayadere
carpet, several kilims… Best not to overlook
the floor in the hallway; a rug can dampen
the noise.

ADD STORAGE CUPBOARDS

Useful for storing all sorts of things, they
can also hold coats and hats. We like them as
discreet as possible, to give more prominence
to paintings and decorative objects.

THE ATTIC

The worst thing to do with space under the roof is to ignore it. Lots of people make the attic into a storage space or playroom. I like to make it into a "living space," a bit like a second living room.

MAKE THE BEST USE OF SPACE
The attic is full of interesting nooks you can use to their fullest. I usually remove false ceilings and partitions to expose the roof structure.

TAKE CARE OF THE BEAMS
If the structural elements are superb, leave them in their natural state or paint them a contrasting color (for instance, the beams black, the walls white) to incorporate them into the decorative scheme. Otherwise, I generally paint them the same color as the walls to eliminate the rustic aspect.

THINK CUSTOM-MADE
If there's ever a place where it makes sense to put in custom-built elements, this is it! Adding cupboards at the foot of a sloping wall and in a corner provides valuable storage space.

ADAPT THE FURNITURE
Does the attic have a low ceiling? Bring in seats, sofas, and armchairs with low backs, which will make the room feel more spacious.

ALLOW FOR DIFFERENT USES
Playroom, piano practice room, television room, office, or guest room... Vary the use by having adaptable furniture and a somewhat chic decorative scheme.

GIVE SOME THOUGHT TO THE LIGHTING
You might use a few spotlights to show off the beams, but otherwise you'll want to avoid hanging light fixtures. Movable lamps are best for altering the ambience.

THE STAIRS

For me, the décor of a stairwell gets as much attention as a main room, if you're lucky enough to have a house or an apartment with two stories!

CHOOSE THE RIGHT MATERIALS

I'm a great fan of staircases whose structure is exposed, especially if they're made of wood or metal. A nice staircase looks like a work of art.

PUT IT ON DISPLAY

You don't hide a staircase; you highlight it. In my own house, I've made a bright blue wall behind the staircase so it's even more visible! But it also works to have a little stairwell painted black or white, making it seem almost like a box or an airlock.

A RUG OR NOT?

Should you have a rug on the stairs or not? It depends on what you want and how you live. Four kids who race around the house? Better have a rug. Just a couple? Not really necessary. I like striped rugs, which add an interesting geometrical element, especially when the stairs are all white. When the stripes run in the same direction as the stairs, they accentuate their effect. Another choice is to paint the risers and the railing black and to leave the treads their natural wood color.

Decorate, decorate, decorate

Whenever I have a staircase, I take the
opportunity to mount photographs, paintings, mirrors. . . .

THE

Bedroom

You spend more time in the bedroom than anywhere else in the house! For me, it's an essential space, one where I can find peace, and I treat it with as much attention as all the other rooms—maybe more.

MY ESSENTIALS

I do everything on my bed: read, play with the children, talk to my friends on the phone, watch TV, prepare for meetings, design furniture, eat, work on my computer.... Sleep? Sure, that too. But not a lot!

A GOOD BED

A hard, firm bed or a squishy, soft one? Everyone has her own philosophy when it comes to the perfect bed! Mine is big—very big (80 × 80 inches [200 × 200 cm]), so I can share it with my newspapers, my children (who gather there to clown around), my computer, my meal tray.... I like being comfortable when I sleep!

MY MATTRESS

It's a Tempur-Pedic, made of memory foam (www.tempurpedic.com). The material was developed for the berths of NASA astronauts. Responsive to heat, it molds to your contours while supporting you perfectly. A good night's sleep is guaranteed!

USE A MATTRESS TOPPER OR NOT?

I like mattress toppers once in a while, when I'm spending a night in a hotel, but at home I prefer not having one. Be careful of the down ones, which can prick you if they're of poor quality.

MY PILLOWS

I have four of them on my bed, two square
ones (25 × 25 inches [65 × 65 cm])
in the back and two rectangular ones
(20 × 28 inches [50 × 70 cm]) in the front.
It's more comfortable for reading or working
in bed. But when I sleep, I use just one rectangular pillow. A pillow can be traditional
(down, feathers, latex, buckwheat husks, or
wool), memory foam, or synthetic (polyester,
microfiber). To each their own. Me, I tend
to like down-filled pillows. The thing to
know? You have to change pillows every
year because the down gets compacted. I
even have clients who change them every six
months—and inscribe the date of purchase
on each pillow!

MY SHEETS

Always white! I like their fresh look. And
I'm partial to cotton percale and, for the
children, stonewashed linen. My fantasy? A
colored welt cord, or some white-on-white
embroidery . . .

MY BLANKETS

Since I sleep under a quilt, I don't really
need an extra blanket. That said, I like to
have a tartan rug, a quilted bedspread, or a
cashmere throw at the foot of the bed. It's
pretty, comfortable, and perfect for a nap. My
favorites are made of cashmere or merino
wool, a solid color, two-colored, or with a
discreet design.

MY ACCESSORIES

Next to my bed, I can't do without my newspapers, my laptop, my books, my scented
candle, and, of course, my iPhone charger.
People say it's bad for you to sleep next to
your phone, but I have to have it there. The
first thing I do when I wake up is turn it on!
The key is to have an attractive place to keep
everything.

STYLE YOUR BEDROOM

Making your bedroom look chic is easy!

SOME ART

Opening your eyes and seeing something beautiful every day puts you in a good mood first thing in the morning. I like to have a painting or a photograph above the bed, a big beautiful piece that draws your eye. On the other walls, I enjoy mixing family snapshots and signed prints.

SOME COLOR

A colored headboard, doors and moldings highlighted in blue or black, a painted section of the wall behind the bed, a brightly colored bed covering... A few flashes of color around the room will give it more depth.

An artistic headboard

This magnificent mural sculpture was made by
Zoé Ouvrier. It's almost as if the headboard has
been replaced with a work of art.

GOOD LIGHTING

Forget about lighting a bedroom with a
ceiling fixture, or, even worse, with spotlights! It kills the ambience. The best is to
have two bedside lamps, plus, ideally, a
discreet pair of LED reading lights. And why
not, one or two standing lamps or table lamps
as well. You can have little islands of light
scattered everywhere.

AN ARMCHAIR

This is crucial! I always have a cozy armchair
in my bedroom where I can curl up and read
or throw my clothes. Or maybe a love seat
punched up with a few colored pillows.

A RUG

You want softness in a bedroom. It can be a pile carpet or a pretty rug laid over the parquet floor. My favorites? Lambswool Berber tribal rugs with geometric designs, from the mountainous Azilal region of Morocco.

THE BEDSIDE TABLE

It's my companion during the day and at night.
It's worth choosing carefully.

On my nightstand, you'll find:

* A lamp

* A scented candle—yes, even there!

* A handsome photograph

* A jar of night cream

* A book

* An alarm clock

* A box of tissues

A REAL NIGHTSTAND

Some people use a chair, a stool... It looks nice in photographs, but it's not very handy. Better to have a real nightstand. I like them on the high side and with a drawer, because you always have stuff that's personal or unattractive that you want to hide.

NATURAL MATERIALS

I hate plastic and plywood. For my bedside, I choose wood, glass, or metal.

GOOD IDEA: A BUILT-IN HEADBOARD

If the room is really small, a built-in headboard can be a good way to gain space. You can put pictures on it, lamps, books...

WHAT ABOUT BOOKS?

A house needs to have books everywhere. Even in the bedroom.

BOOKCASES

Book storage in a bedroom? Why not? Especially in the children's rooms. In my own room, I prefer not to have a ton of bookcases with novels and paperbacks. To keep dust from gathering, I like a relatively spare environment. But I make an exception for shelves inside floor-level cupboards, where books can be stored out of sight.

A TABLE

Tables and consoles are my best friends! In the bedroom, I always have one where I can put my favorite reading materials, novels and coffee-table books. I use them to make a kind of horizontal mood board. It looks nice, it's stylish, and it's easy.

STACK THEM HIGH

Piles of books, especially large illustrated books, are colorful items that can punctuate a decorative scheme like so many architectural elements.

DRESS UP YOUR WINDOWS

Curtains or blinds? The two camps are generally at a standoff.

But I get along with everyone. I use both.

THE ART OF SHEER CURTAINS

Out of favor for a long time, sheer curtains are making a comeback. But beware! Not just any will do. They have to be of a natural material— gauze or lightweight linen—to provide a screen without blocking the light.

EFFICIENT BLINDS

In the bedroom, I like to have blinds to protect my privacy. Made to measure, they quietly provide isolation.

CURTAINS

Yes, yes, yes! A room needs curtains. First, because you sleep better in the dark, so line the curtains with lightproof cloth. And second, because they warm up the room's tone. My favorite styles? Flemish pleats, flat pleats, and pinch pleats, which should be made by a professional. For the fabric, I like coarse linens, cotton, and velvet, and all of one color, preferably. I buy my curtain rods at Le BHV Marais (52 rue de Rivoli, 75004 Paris; www.bhv.fr/en).

I adore...

* **Rue Hérold:** Decorated in all white and very chic, the store carries a wonderful selection of strikingly contemporary fabrics. Interior decorator Charlotte de la Grandière is the driving force, and she favors high-end fabrics made of natural materials (linen, cotton duck, China grass cloth, wool) and sober colors: blues, blacks, grays, whites, ecrus, and beiges. Best of all, the shop carries ready-made curtains and a collection of curtain rods.
8 rue Hérold, 75001 Paris; tel. +33 01 42 33 66 56; www.rueherold.fr

My useful addresses

HOUSEHOLD LINENS

* **D. Porthault:** This essential luxury brand is made with sublime materials and elaborate embroidery.
5 rue de Boccador, 75008 Paris; tel. +33 01 84 17 27 37
Find retail outlets at www.dporthault.fr/home?lang=en_EN

* **Olivier Desforges:** Beautiful things at affordable prices.
94 rue Saint-Antoine, 75004 Paris; tel. +33 01 42 72 11 03
Find retail outlets at en.olivierdesforges.fr

* **Descamps:** Good basics.
28 rue d'Aboukir, 75002 Paris; tel. +33 01 53 32 27 00
Find retail outlets at www.descamps.com

* **Linvosges:** Table linen specialists.
33 rue Saint-Placide, 75006 Paris; tel. +33 01 42 97 49 81
Find retail outlets at www.linvosges.com

* **Le Bon Marché:** All the major brands at good prices.
24 rue de Sèvres, 75007 Paris; tel. +33 01 44 39 80 00
www.lebonmarche.com/en.html

* **AM.PM.:** The high-end brand of the La Redoute chain, presently with one store in Paris.
77 rue de Charonne, 75011 Paris; tel. +33 01 47 00 02 20
International delivery available at www.laredoute.com

* **Carré Blanc**
78 rue Montmartre, 75002 Paris; tel. +33 01 40 13 70 33
Order online at www.carreblanc.com

ALSO:

* **Merci:** For stonewashed linen sheets.
111 boulevard Beaumarchais, 75003 Paris; tel. +33 01 42 77 00 33
Shop online at www.merci-merci.com/en

* **No-Mad:** A company with a superb line of bed linens designed by Valérie Barkowski, a Frenchwoman, and Anuj Kothari, who is from Mumbai.
Shop online at www.no-mad.in

* **Hamam:** Its bed linens and bath linens are upmarket and prettily finished.
23 rue Tronchet, 75008 Paris; tel. +33 01 42 72 36 39
Shop online at www.hamam.eu/en

* **Tensira:** Sumptuous pillows and sheets in indigo-dyed African cotton.
21 place des Vosges, 75004 Paris; tel. +33 09 83 87 93 10
www.tensira.com/index.php?lang=en

* **Brun de Vian-Tiran:** A French luxury brand since 1808, it sells fine blankets made of cashmere, camelhair, alpaca, and mohair.
Find retail outlets or shop online at www.brundeviantiran.com/en/brand-blanket-prestige-natural-fibres.cfm

* **Hermès:** An extravagance! But one that will last a lifetime.
24 rue du Faubourg Saint-Honoré, 75008 Paris; tel. +33 01 40 17 46 00
Find retail outlets or shop online at www.hermes.com/index_us.html

* **By Mölle:** Spare, modern basics for plaid blankets, and also sheets and pillows.
tel. +31 5 29 46 69 65
Shop online at www.bymolle.com

* **Foxford Woollen Mills:** An Irish company with lovely checkered blankets.
tel. +35 3 94 92 56 104
Shop online at www.foxfordwoollenmills.com

* **Studio Mae Engelgeer:** A Dutch manufacturer of poetic, modern tartan rugs and blankets.
tel. +31 6 10 89 79 14
Shop online at www.mae-engelgeer.nl

* **Oyuna:** Exceptional cashmere homegoods presented by a young woman from Mongolia, Oyuna Tserendorj.
tel. +44 20 71 83 93 03
Shop online at www.oyuna.com

THE

Bathroom

It's my bubble, the place where I can draw breath,
where I prepare myself and recharge my batteries.
I've made it into a cocoon, cozy and relaxing.
A place where my children often join me!

An XXL candle for a scented atmosphere.

A mini-sized perfume bottle perfect for slipping into your handbag. The monogrammed case makes it even better.

Cement tiles are a relatively traditional material that I use to give the floor a patterned, contemporary look.

There is nothing better than enameled lava tiles for reflecting light and creating extraordinarily beautiful and very subtle colors.

I never hesitate to use marble. It's a pure, elegant material.

My lucky ring from Stone Paris.

I like to bring the bathroom to life using elegant, refined materials.

MY ESSENTIALS

The room may be utilitarian, but it still needs to be given serious thought and decorated. I spend enough time in the bathroom that I like to make it a place for conducting my life—to the point that I telephone from the bathtub!

AN ARMCHAIR

Why an armchair in the bathroom? It's a place to park your bathrobe, it gives the space a touch of the boudoir, and it lets you hold a conversation with someone while you take your bath. There's always a chair, an armchair, or even a little bench in my bathrooms. The ideal? Something not too fragile: wicker, wood, coarse cotton fabric . . .

MUSIC PLAYER

I absolutely must have music! So I always make room for a radio in the bathroom. Even better, a speaker I can plug my iPhone into so I can listen to my playlists.

A BATHROBE

The only thing I dry with a towel is my hair. When I emerge from the bath, I wrap myself in a white terry-cloth bathrobe from Chez Zoé and raise the hood. I can't think of anything cozier. I have the children's bathrobes embroidered with their names, or I attach a colored tassel to them.

CANDLES

You already know how crazy I am about candles. . . . So, obviously, I put some in the bathroom. Two options: a scented candle, or a cluster of wax candles with electric flames for an elegant ambience.

PERFUME

I've been loyal since adolescence to Obsession by Calvin Klein, which my father used to bring back for me from the United States. I always wear it in the wintertime. During the summer, I move on to Mûre et Musc by l'Artisan Parfumeur, which my daughter, Yasmine, is now also wearing. Recently, I've fallen in love with the perfumes of Atelier Cologne, particularly Orange Sanguine and Grand Néroli.

LUXURY SOAPS

The delicately scented soaps of Frédéric Malle are the best! They smell incredibly good and rinse off easily. When I travel, I always carry one with me.

BATH TOWELS

I may not use them to dry myself, but I obviously have bath towels in my bathroom. Always of terry cloth, always white, always bought from Chez Zoé, sometimes trimmed with color.

WHERE TO BUY BATH LINENS

* **Chez Zoé:** Beautiful custom embroidery made in Morocco by two very friendly sisters.
20 rue Cambon, 75001 Paris;
tel. +33 01 44 50 78 12
www.chezzoe.com

* **Uchino:** A Japanese brand offering towels that are terry cloth on one side and a cotton print (dots, lines) on the other, in subtle colors.
Available at Le Bon Marché Rive Gauche, 24 rue de Sèvres, Paris 75007;
tel. +33 01 44 39 80 00
www.lebonmarche.com/en.html
Find retailers and shop online at www.uchino.co.jp/en/

* **Hamam:** Its bed linens and bath linens are upmarket and prettily finished.
23 rue Tronchet, 75008 Paris;
tel. +33 01 42 72 36 39
Shop online at www.hamam.eu/tr_en

* **Descamps:** Good basics.
28 rue d'Aboukir, 75002 Paris;
tel. +33 01 53 32 27 00
Find retail outlets at www.descamps.com

* **AM.PM.:** The high-end brand of La Redoute, presently with one store in Paris.
77 rue de Charonne, 75011 Paris;
tel. +33 01 47 00 02 20
International delivery available at www.laredoute.com

READY IN TEN MINUTES

I'm not a beauty treatment addict, I don't own thousands of beauty products, I wear minimal makeup, and I don't spend hours in front of my mirror. All of that shows me to be a true Parisienne, since it's often said that a Parisian woman's chic comes from being extravagantly natural. But I have the good fortune to have professionals visit my home and work nearby. Here are my secrets, and theirs!

HAIR

The key is to get a haircut that looks great
and takes no time to maintain. For me
it's an artfully tousled look, for which I
am indebted to Delphine Courteille, a
talented hairstylist and hairdresser with a
well-known salon: Le Studio 34 (34 rue du
Mont Thabor, 75001 Paris; tel. +33 01 47 03 35 35;
www.delphinecourteille.com).

She cuts my hair every three or four
months on average, feathering it in front
to get the hair away from my face.

Tips from Delphine Courteille:

* For Sarah, I've chosen 1970s-style bangs,
long and feathered, natural.

* I mix together three tones of blond in
Sarah's hair (honey, beige, and gold) to
give her a sunstruck look.

* I advise her to avoid all shampoos
containing silicone, which make
hair heavy.

* I recommend that she dry her hair with
a towel, avoiding the hair dryer, which
can flatten hair. The only exception is
in brushing out her bangs, to give them
lightness and style.

* Once a month, a macadamia oil
treatment to repair dry and damaged
strands.

The products I use:

* Opalis cream shampoo and conditioner

* Beauty cream with macadamia oil by
Biorène for nourishing my hair

* A large roller for rolling my bangs
ten minutes before going out, to give
them volume

MAKEUP

There's no way I can spend hours in front of the mirror or put on sophisticated makeup on a daily basis! In the morning, if I don't have a one-on-one meeting, I apply a dab of face cream, a little mascara, and a stroke of eyeliner pencil. Done! At night, I go a little further. And for fancy occasions, photo shoots, or glamorous dinners, I call on Mayu Yamaji, a makeup artist for Delphine Courteille, who transforms me in a few minutes.

Tips from Mayu:

* Sarah has a wonderful complexion; there's no need to do a lot of work on it.

* To use as little foundation as possible, I moisten her skin with cream and massage her face for a few minutes. That takes the place of a makeup base.

* I start by brushing back her eyelashes, before applying brown eyeliner for daytime and a mix of brown and black for night. I finish with black mascara.

* For radiance of skin tone, I work with a light-colored white-pink Nars makeup stick, applying it to the corners of her eyes and the tops of her cheekbones.

* Sarah has a naturally healthy glow, so she doesn't need much blush or bronzer. A little rose blush is enough.

* Sarah likes having natural lips. A nice, transparent lip moistener, and she's good to go!

HAND CARE

I like my hands to be impeccable, and I like heightening their effect with color. That's why Kamel, a wonderful manicurist, comes to the house once a week. It's my personal luxury! Appointments via kamelmanucure@gmail.com.

Tips from Kamel:

* Sarah wears her nails short and neat, never long.

* To repair her hands and nails, I give her an oil made of jasmine, argan, and lemon. It moisturizes, and it transports you to foreign lands!

* Sarah is pretty rock and roll. I apply a red-orange polish by Yves Saint Laurent to her toenails. She likes her fingernails a less conventional color: greens, deep blues, sometimes burgundy . . . but never a pale color.

My products:

* Embryolisse Micellar Lotion, as a skin cleanser

* The silky moisturizing cream Régénération Intense by Crème de la Mer, which gives exceptional results

* Foundation by Shu Uemura in a compact, for its delicate finish

* Golden beige Touche Éclat highlighter from Yves Saint Laurent, for its subtle shades

* By Terry kohl, a highly natural eyeliner

* Volume by Une mascara

THINK OF YOURSELF

No need to spend hours pampering yourself to feel good.
A few tricks will help you feel years younger!

TAKE A BATH

I jump into the bathtub every morning to wake up slowly. Hot and foamless, that's how I like it! I may be a Pisces, but aside from my bathtub, I hate bathing in swimming pools or spas. I make an exception for swimming in the ocean, at Cap Ferret, when it's not too cold!

DRINK GREEN TEA

I'm not a stickler for organic food. I smoke, I eat candy, red meat.... But I am a serious drinker of green tea from Japan, all through the day.

TREAT YOURSELF TO A HEAD MASSAGE

It feels crazy good! Emmanuel Roy makes home visits and gives unbelievable scalp massages using coconut oil. I offer myself this luxury when I'm totally beat: I come away feeling great and my hair looks better too! A telephone number that is worth gold:
+33 06 84 41 57 85; www.emmanuelroy.sitew.fr

TAKE UP BOXING

I box with a coach, either at home or in the Tuileries Gardens if it's nice out. Recently, I've taken up Bodytech, an electronic system that improves your flexibility, muscle tone, and balance.

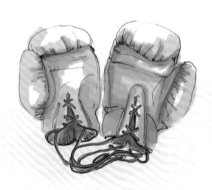

MY BONUS TIPS

We all dream of having the perfect bathroom.... And if you have these elements you are well on your way.

PLENTY OF CUPBOARDS
A bathroom is more attractive when it's not cluttered with stuff. This is even truer when several people share the bathroom. I always try to make sure that there will be enough cupboards for lots and lots of things, preferably cupboards that melt into the background.

A RUG OF THE RIGHT KIND
Some like duckboards at the door to the shower. In a weekend home, why not? But in my apartment, I'd rather have a woven cotton rug, which has the advantage of drying faster than terry cloth.

NO TOYS
On no condition is the bathroom to be awash in toys. If the room has to be shared with children, then you restrict the number of toys allowed and they must be put away in cupboards after use.

ATTRACTIVE CONTAINERS

Of course, there will be stuff lying out in plain sight. The trick is to store it attractively. A lovely pencil jar for brushes and makeup. Wicker or rattan baskets for jars of moisturizer and hairbrushes. Wooden boxes (Ikea, Habitat, The Conran Shop) for perfumes, creams, accessories . . .

A STYLISH MIRROR

Two options: Cover a section of wall with a mirror or mount a large hanging mirror. The second solution can be more creative than the first and give the room character, especially if you find a good secondhand mirror, something a little original.

GOOD LIGHTING

Forget spotlights on the ceiling that make your complexion look terrible, your eyes hollow, and your pimples gigantic! The ideal is soft lighting: wall lights on either side of the mirror.

A BIG SHOWER

I adore Italian showers, extra large, with overhead rain panels or big showerheads. But what I dream of having is a little hamam right in my house.

PHOTOGRAPHS ON THE WALL

Just because the room is utilitarian doesn't
mean you shouldn't decorate it! I have lots
of framed family photos in my bathroom,
vacation snaps, travel pics.... I don't put art
photographs there, but life photographs.

A GOOD BATHTUB

This is important to me! I hate acrylic
bathtubs, which look too "plastic-y." I prefer
tubs of enameled steel, such as those from
Boffi. A good idea is to buy an old-fashioned
claw-foot bathtub and paint the outside of
it for an inexpensive and colorful effect. It
doesn't have to be a sunken tub!

RADIANT HEAT

Because it's super comfortable for someone
like me, who walks around barefoot a lot! But
it doesn't keep me from installing towel-
warming radiators too.

RAW MATERIALS

It's often said that what makes a bathroom beautiful is the quality

of its materials. It's partly true....

SHOULD YOU USE WOOD?

Why not? Whatever people may say, using wood in a bathroom is not heresy. It just needs to be treated correctly with several coats of marine varnish to protect it from humidity. I'm very fond of bathrooms all in natural oak—walls, floor, and counters.

WHAT TILES TO CHOOSE?

Cement tiles can be a good choice for a bathroom, particularly for the floor. Their patterns are stylish, and they develop a patina with age. Another option is to install large stoneware floor tiles, which are sturdy and practical. Many closely imitate marble or granite. If your budget is tight, there's nothing like 4 × 4-inch (10 × 10 cm) white tiles on the walls and stone (or stoneware) on the floor.

WHAT DO I THINK OF MARBLE?

I like it! I love marble in a bathroom, especially when it's installed everywhere, on the floor and the walls for a "box" or cocoon effect. But I like it better when it's not polished, but simply smoothed for a matte finish. I'm also very fond of Hainaut bluestone from Belgium. Slate, on the other hand, while very beautiful, quickly develops marks from calcium. Better to imitate slate with stoneware tiles. With marble and Burgundy stone, be sure to treat it correctly to avoid staining.

SHOULD YOU USE GLASS MOSAIC TILES?

Yes, on condition that the mosaics are small (½ × ½ inches [1 × 1 cm]), which are prettier in a bathroom. And a single color. I'm not a fan of designs on the walls.

THUMBS-UP OR THUMBS-DOWN ON TADELAKT?

Tadelakt, the traditional wall coating for hamams and bathrooms in Morocco, is fine in a vacation home, but not in an apartment. A tadelakt coating is quite fragile, and when buildings shift, as they do in Paris, it can crack.

WHAT'S THE BEST THING FOR A CHILDREN'S BATHROOM?

Super-sturdy materials! Marble is out, stone is out, mosaic is out. Very durable tiles and nothing else. We prefer neutral tones. Most patterns quickly grow tiresome, especially those created for children. And you don't want to be redoing the bathroom all the time.

CHOOSING FAUCETS

Once again, let's hear it for restraint! No point in being original with plumbing fixtures; it's best to choose something that's going to last. I like them classic, neutral, chic, and of high quality.

THE
Wardrobe

Fashion is a world I fell into when I was practically
a child: My father was the longtime director of
Vogue, and my mother and grandmother were
women of absolute elegance.

MY ESSENTIALS

The most important thing for me is to feel good... and quickly!

So I have a "day uniform": jeans, shirt, and sneakers or men's boots.

At night, a different uniform: heels, a minidress, and a dinner jacket...

WINTER

* Well-cut jeans, and I like them low-waisted and body-hugging. I choose slightly faded ones.

* Loose-fitting cashmere sweaters with a wide or V-shaped neckline. Comfort comes first! I favor grays, blues, blacks, whites....

* Shirts with checks, solid colors, or discreet patterns. They are absolute basics for me.

* A man's coat or a leather jacket.

* Oxfords and ankle boots, always on the boyish side. My favorite brand: Church's, which has very pretty shoes for women. Expensive, but they last.

* Scarves, the bigger the better, which I can wrap around myself for protection from the cold.

* Super-soft lambskin gloves.

FASHION JUST A CLICK AWAY

Because the day has only twenty-four hours, I'm all for shopping online. The moment I can spare a minute, I'll surf the web and buy, sometimes while multitasking.

Here are my favorite fashion sites:

* Sézane: www.sezane.com/en
* L'Exception: www.lexception.com/en
* Olive Clothing: www.oliveclothing.com
* Shopbop: www.shopbop.com
* Net-a-Porter: www.net-a-porter.com
* Mytheresa.com: www.mytheresa.com/en-us

THE BEST ACCESSORIES

I'm not always eager to own the latest trendy handbags. I prefer a good basic design, elegant and timeless, which I generally wear with a shoulder strap. And I don't own a large handbag for lugging my life around in. A bag that can hold my purse, telephone, cigarettes, and keys does the trick for me.

SUMMER

My favorite season! Because it's easy to be cool, you naturally look healthy, and the clothes are ultra-light.

* Good shorts. This is THE basic item for summer! They can be denim (see my favorite jeans brands, page 138) or made of white, blue, or beige cotton. Same for simple cotton pants.

* A bathing suit, or several, even—two-piece triangle bikinis only. I generally buy a swimsuit every year from Erès and then another, but not quite as classic, while I'm on vacation.

* T-shirts of washed cotton, soft, with a wide V-neck. I wear them almost every day.

* Some light shirts.

* Sunglasses with a little style, like the Michel Klein collection by Gipsy Caravan.

* Greek sandals of natural leather.

* Sneakers, usually white, in either leather or fabric.

MY HOME OUTFIT

What do I love to wear when I'm cocooning at home? A track suit. It sounds terrible, but there are some very handsome ones in cotton or flannel, subdued and elegant. I buy them at Sundry, James Perse, and Journal Standard Luxe.

24 HOURS WITHOUT A CHANGE OF CLOTHES

Impossible is not a fashion word! Elegance is not a function of how much time you spend in your dressing room. And just because you work during the day and shuttle between your kids' lives and your own is no reason not to be elegant at night. Stepping up to Cinderella 2.0 is perfectly doable!

MY PUMPS

Like my mother, I adore high heels, even if I don't wear them every day—far from it. The shoe designer I've really fallen for is Gianvito Rossi. I am literally crazy about his shoes.

SETTING OFF FULLY EQUIPPED

What's a simple way to transform your look? By changing shoes. Replace your Greek sandals or your sneakers with a pair of stilettos, and you've changed everything! I can't walk all day on a pair of four-inch heels—but at night, I can. Even if I don't change out of my jeans. So I always keep a pair of simple black pumps in a drawer at the office, and off I go!

GO FOR JEWELRY

Although I don't wear earrings, I like rings—openwork rings like those by Bucellati, and necklaces, including ones sprinkled with little stones, from Stone Paris, a brand started by my sister, Marie.

PUT ON A SKIRT

A dress or skirt + heels + a shirt + a jacket + a clutch = an evening look that is modern and simple.

TREAT YOURSELF TO A (FINE) JACKET

A nicely tailored and close-fitting jacket structures your outline and instantly gives you a boyish touch of elegance. It's modern and not girlish. That's why I love jackets.

SARAH, AS SEEN BY . . .

MARIE PONIATOWSKI

* **Founder of the jewelry line Stone Paris and my sister!**

If Sarah were an item of clothing? *A Saint Laurent jacket.*
An accessory? *A superb pair of high-heeled shoes by Gianvito Rossi.*
A theater or movie costume? *Angélique's costume in Marquise*
des Anges.
If she were going to a costume party, how would you dress her?
As Wonder Woman, which she is.
And for an evening party? *An Alexandre Vauthier gown, with pumps by*
Gianvito Rossi: too sexy!
What item of clothing will she never be able to wear? *She can wear anything, but I have*
trouble imagining her in a culotte skirt!
And the hairdo or makeup that will never suit her? *Pigtails, and fuchsia pink lipstick.*
And the item of clothing that she'll still look great in at eighty? *Her jeans.*

MADEMOISELLE AGNÈS

* **Free spirit and icon of the fashion world**

If Sarah were an item of clothing? *A piece of fabric, at least twelve inches*
above the knee.
An accessory? *Her long blond hair.*
A theater or movie costume? *The Bionic Woman's cool khaki jumpsuit.*
If she were going to a costume party, how would you dress her?
As a smiley.
For an evening party? *Her smile is all she needs.*
And the hairdo or makeup that will never suit her? *Lipstick.*
And the item of clothing that she'll still be wearing at eighty? *Her watch and*
her friends.

AUDREY MARNAY

* **Actress**

If Sarah were an item of clothing? *A tuxedo jacket.*
An accessory? *A gold cuff from Tiffany.*
A theater or movie costume? *Peter Pan.*
How would you dress her for an evening party? *As Empress Elisabeth*
(Sisi) of Austria.
What item of clothing will she never be able to wear? *Bell-bottoms.*
And the hairdo that will never suit her? *A ladylike chignon.*
And the item of clothing that she'll still be wearing at eighty? *Her*
little black jacket.

VERONIQUE PHILIPPONNAT

⋆ Journalist

If Sarah were an item of clothing? *Any old thing, since she looks great in any old thing.*

An accessory? *The arm of the man she loves!*

A famous person? *Olympe de Gouges, because she's much more of a feminist than you think.*

A movie costume? *Jeanne Moreau's costume in Jules et Jim: a black suit and a penciled mustache.*

If you had to disguise her for a costume party, how would you dress her? *As the Khaleesi in* Game of Thrones.

For an intimate dinner? *Just as she is, but right before going out, a roller for her bangs!*

And for an evening party? *A G7 taxi and great long legs coming out the passenger door. That's all!*

The item of clothing she'll never be able to wear? *A velvet hairband, maybe?*

And the item of clothing that will still suit her when she's eighty? *Her laugh, recognizable among a thousand others.*

VANESSA SEWARD

⋆ Fashion designer

If Sarah were an item of clothing? *A glam minidress, a skinny pair of jeans, or a blazer.*

An accessory? *A pair of boots.*

A famous person? *She is famous!*

A moment when you found Sarah particularly beautiful? *Every time I see her I notice how well she has mastered that deceptive look of relaxed elegance.*

If you had to disguise her for a costume party, how would you dress her? *As a grande dame of the old school, on the order of Edmonde Charles-Roux.*

And for an evening party? *In a minidress; she has spectacular legs.*

In what way is Sarah a Parisienne? *She never looks dressed up; she wears her evening clothes as though they were jeans.*

EMMANUELLE ALT

⋆ Editor in chief of Paris *Vogue*

If Sarah were an item of clothing? *A miniskirt or shorts, because she has stunning legs!*

An accessory? *A lighter, because she smokes a great deal (too much).*

A famous person? *Brigitte Bardot, because she's effortlessly beautiful, goes barefoot, and has tanned legs and tousled blond hair.*

If you had to disguise her for a costume party, how would you dress her? *As Brigitte Bardot, it would be easy, or in Mireille Darc's black dress* in The Tall Blond Man with One Black Shoe.

For an intimate dinner? *Jeans and a white T-shirt.*

And for an evening party? *A Pleats Please by Issey Miyake.*

An item of clothing she'll never be able to wear? *Short hair and red lipstick.*

What will she still wear when she is eighty? *Everything will still look great on her, except the shorts, which she'll have stopped wearing around age seventy-eight.*

The last time you laughed together? *Every morning, when we call each other at 8:20 A.M.*

CÉCILIA BÖNSTRÖM

* **Artistic director of Zadig et Voltaire**

If Sarah were an item of clothing? *A white T-shirt. She projects such style she doesn't need anything more.*
An accessory? *A crossbody bag, because she has "coolitude."*
A famous person? *Françoise Sagan, because they are both real Parisiennes.*
A theater or movie costume? *An officer's jacket, for her masculine-feminine side.*
If you had to disguise her for a costume party, how would you dress her? *As a fairy, on account of her eternally young look.*
For an evening party? *Black jeans and black blazer, ultra-feminine shoes.*
And for an intimate dinner? *A lingerie-type silk top, jeans, and sneakers.*
What item of clothing will she never be able to wear? *An ankle-length flower-print dress.*
And the hairdo or makeup that will never suit her? *Anything too sophisticated!*
And the item of clothing she will still wear at eighty? *Her white T-shirt, still.*

ROMAN

* **My son, eight years old**

If Sarah were an item of clothing? *A Saint Laurent jacket, because she wears one all the time.*
An accessory? *Her iPhone.*
A famous person? *Cinderella, because they have the same hair.*
A movie costume? *A gladiator's costume.*
If you had to disguise her for a costume party, how would you dress her? *She would be naked, with a huge Sarah Lavoine logo!*
For an intimate dinner? *She'd wear gold glasses with stars on them, pointy shoes, and kneesocks. She'd be the center of attention.*
And for an evening party? *As herself.*
What item of clothing will she never be able to wear? *A necktie and a Mohawk hairdo.*
What will she still be wearing when she is eighty? *Underwear.*

YASMINE

* **My daughter, seventeen years old**

If Sarah were an item of clothing? *A T-shirt or the smock designed for Swildens.*
An accessory? *Her pink Jil Sander oxfords that I'm always stealing from her closet.*
A famous person? *Madonna in Desperately Seeking Susan, she's funny and completely crazy.*
If you had to disguise her for a costume party, how would you dress her? *As Betty Boop, because she'd be completely different.*
For an intimate dinner? *Totally chill! White shirt, black jeans, gold belt.*
And for an evening party? *A Masai minidress by Michel Klein.*
The item that she'll never be able to wear? *Cowboy boots!*
What will she still wear when she is eighty? *Her Azzaro dress designed by Vanessa Seward, black with gold dots.*
The last time you laughed together? *Too many to remember, she's my mother!*

Tuxedo Function

"The tuxedo jacket belongs to style, not to fashion.... Fashions fade, style is eternal," said Saint Laurent. I agree with him 100 percent. The tuxedo is a basic element of my wardrobe. It goes with everything, day and night. It works with jeans, with dressy pants, lamé shorts, a dress, even a smock. It's masculine and also totally feminine. Much sexier for me than a minidress! I can't think of a more adaptable, more practical item of clothing. I like it tailored, form-fitting, the way Hedi Slimane at Saint Laurent knows how to do so well.

SORT YOUR CLOTHES BY COLOR

A dressing room is first of all a useful space. And it obviously consists mostly of closets. There are more glamorous parts of the house. Of course, if you have the room, you can bring in an armchair, a mirror, pretty light fixtures.... But the important thing is to organize your clothes.

SEASONS AND CLOTHES

There are several schools of thought on how to organize a wardrobe. You don't need an advanced degree in folding to suspect that the point is to keep things organized. Some like to have a summer section and a winter section. It does make life easier. Others sort according to the type of clothing: shirts, pants, dresses, shoes. I'm OK with that too! As I am with anything that makes life simpler.

HURRAY FOR COLOR!

It may not be a high-traffic area (though some women may spend hours there), but you should still pay attention to its decoration. I sort my clothes by color and shade. So, I'll put all the blues together, then sort them from dark to light.

AN EFFICIENT WEEKEND BAG

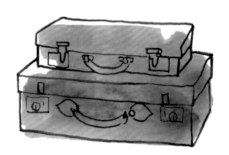

Every weekend, I set off for the country. And I often hop on a train or a plane to spend a few days in another European city, or somewhere farther afield. Naturally, I've become a pro at packing! Here are some tips.

LIST WHAT YOU'LL NEED

It sounds obvious, but you don't need the same stuff on a romantic weekend in Venice that you'll need to hack through the fields in the country. Start by asking yourself what the weekend's activities will be. Then bring the elements together.

WEEKEND IN THE COUNTRY (SUMMER)

A pair of sneakers + a pair of sandals + a pair of shorts + cotton pants + three T-shirts + a cashmere sweater + a scarf + underwear + a toilet kit + sunglasses

URBAN WEEKEND TRIP (SUMMER)

A pair of sneakers + sandals + high heels + shorts + jeans + a skirt + three T-shirts + a cashmere sweater + a scarf + a nice jacket + underwear + a toilet kit + sunglasses + a few pieces of jewelry

WEEKEND IN THE COUNTRY (WINTER)

A down jacket + sneakers + boots or ankle boots + two pairs of jeans + three long-sleeve T-shirts + two cashmere sweaters + a scarf + underwear + socks + a toilet kit

URBAN WEEKEND TRIP (WINTER)

A nice coat + a sleek down jacket + sneakers + boots or ankle boots + two pairs of jeans + three long-sleeve T-shirts + two cashmere sweaters + a scarf + underwear + socks + a pair of high heels + a toilet kit + a few pieces of jewelry

PACK CAREFULLY

* Fold the T-shirts, shirts, and sweaters to the same size before slipping them into a big cloth bag or a zippered garment bag by Muji.
* Slip the shoes into cloth bags and put them in the bottom of the suitcase.
* The toilet kit also goes in the bottom of the suitcase.
* The more fragile items (silk shirts, dresses, skirts) go on top.
* Try not to have a suitcase that is either half empty (your clothes will shift around) or overly full (everything will get wrinkled). Ideally? Have a set of bags of two or three different sizes so you can choose the right one for the clothes you are taking.

UPON ARRIVAL, EMPTY YOUR BAG

As soon as I arrive at the hotel or the house where I'm staying, I take a few minutes to empty my suitcase and hang up my stuff. It instantly gives you the sense of being at home. Whereas leaving my suitcase half full gets me down!

TAKE GOOD CARE OF YOUR CLOTHES

Carefully choosing your look is good.
Taking good care of your clothes is better.
I may not be a total household wizard, but there
are certain rules I observe.

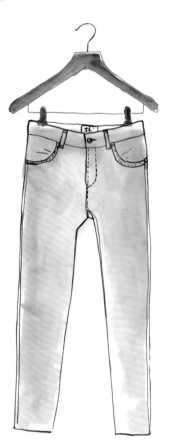

WASH CLOTHES GENTLY

There's no need to wash clothes at a high
temperature or with lots of detergent if the
clothes are not particularly dirty. A heat setting
of 86°F (30°C) on a quick cycle is enough. Be
careful of the spin cycle. A speed of more
than 1,200 rpm can make clothes hard to iron.
As for the dryer, it's practical, but it wears
clothes out.

ALTERNATE WHAT YOU WEAR

It's best to air out one's clothes every day and
not put on the same garment two days running
(this is especially true for wool and cashmere
items). Ditto for shoes.

KEEP DRY CLEANING TO A MINIMUM

Sending clothes to the dry cleaner's is
certainly handy, but it's not really that great
for your health. When clothes come back from
the cleaners, they give off volatile organic
compounds that frankly do you no good. Best
to let the clothes off-gas outside (on the terrace
or a balcony, in the garden) for half an hour
before putting them away in a closet or letting
them hang in your room.

PROTECT YOUR WOOLENS

We're not the only ones who like fine wool
and cashmere. Moths do too! To keep them at
bay without using insecticides, I use blocks of
cedar wood. From time to time, every three
to six months, I sand the blocks down a little
with sandpaper to restore their scent.

My useful addresses

JEANS

* **J Brand:** Available at Printemps department stores
Printemps Haussmann, 64 boulevard Haussmann, 75009 Paris; tel. +33 01 42 82 50 00
departmentstoreparis.printemps.com/en

Find retailers and shop online at www.jbrandjeans.com

* **Current Elliott**
Available at Colette, 213 rue Saint-Honoré, 75001 Paris; tel. +33 01 55 35 33 90
en.colette.fr
Find retailers and shop online at www.currentelliott.com

* **7 for All Mankind**
223 rue Saint-Honoré, 75001 Paris; tel. +33 01 49 26 01 27
Find retailers and shop online at www.7forallmankind.com

* **Acne**
124 galerie de Valois, 75001 Paris; tel. +33 01 42 60 16 62
Find retailers and shop online at www.acnestudios.com

SHIRTS

* **Melinda Gloss**
9 rue Madame, 75006 Paris; tel. +33 01 42 84 31 66
www.melindagloss.com

* **Saint Laurent**
32 rue du Faubourg Saint-Honoré, 75008 Paris; tel. +33 01 53 05 80 80
Find retailers and shop online at www.ysl.com/us

* **French Trotters**
128 rue Vieille-du-Temple, 75003 Paris; tel. +33 01 44 61 00 14
Find retailers at www.frenchtrotters.fr

T-SHIRTS AND OTHER RELAXED ATTIRE

* **Majestic Filatures**
See retail outlets at www.majesticfilatures.com/se/en

* **Journal Standard Luxe**
11–12 galerie de Montpensier, 75001 Paris
Find retailers or shop online at www.journal-standard.jp

* **James Perse**
Available at Colette, 213 rue Saint-Honoré, 75001 Paris; tel. +33 01 55 35 33 90
en.colette.fr
Find retail outlets and shop online at www.jamesperse.com

* **Sundry**
Find retail outlets and shop online at www.sundryclothing.com

* **Isabel Marant**
47 rue de Saintonge, 75003 Paris; tel. +33 01 42 78 19 24
Find retail outlets and shop online at www.isabelmarant.com/en

CASHMERE SWEATERS

* **Leetha**
420 rue Saint-Honoré, 75008 Paris; tel. +33 01 42 61 00 71
www.leetha.fr

* **Éric Bompard**
22 rue Boissy-d'Anglas, Village Royal, 75008 Paris; tel. +33 01 42 68 32 16
Shop online at www.eric-bompard.com/en

* **Zadig et Voltaire**
Find retail outlets and shop at us.zadig-et-voltaire.com

PANTS AND SHORTS

* **Laurence Doligé**
Find retail outlets at www.laurencedolige.com

* **Swildens**
22 rue du Poitou, 75003 Paris; tel. +33 01 42 71 19 12
Shop online at www.swildens.fr/?___store=english&___from_store=fr

COATS

* **Sonia Rykiel**
175 boulevard Saint-Germain, 75006 Paris; tel. +33 01 49 54 60 60
Find retail outlets at www.soniarykiel.com/en_us

* **Balenciaga:** For a well-tailored leather jacket.
336 rue Saint-Honoré, 75001 Paris; tel. +33 01 76 77 37 00
Find retail outlets and shop online at www.balenciaga.com/us

* **Wooyoungmi**
5 rue Saint-Claude, 75003 Paris; tel. +33 01 42 77 85 68
Find retail outlets at www.wooyoungmi.com

SCARVES

* **Épice**
28 galerie de Montpensier, 75001 Paris; tel. +33 01 42 96 68 26
en.epice.com

* **Khadi & Co.**
82 boulevard Beaumarchais, 75011 Paris; tel. +33 01 43 57 10 25
www.khadiandco.com/accueil_en.php

GLOVES

* **Causse**
12 rue de Castiglione, 75006 Paris;
tel. +33 01 49 26 91 43
Shop online at
www.causse-gantier.fr/en

* **Maison Fabre**
128 galerie de Valois, 75001 Paris;
tel. +33 01 42 60 75 88
Shop online at www.maisonfabre.com
/home.php?lang=en

BATHING SUITS

* **Erès**
2 rue Tronchet, 75008 Paris;
tel. +33 01 47 42 28 82
Find retail outlets and shop online at
www.eresparis.com/en

SUNGLASSES

* **Michel Klein**
Available at www.gipsycaravan.com/en

SHOES

* **Gianvito Rossi**
40 rue du Mont-Thabor, 75001 Paris;
tel. +33 01 49 26 96 43
Find retail outlets and shop online at
www.gianvitorossi.com

* **Church's**
229 rue Saint-Honoré, 75001 Paris;
tel. +33 01 55 35 34 60
Find retail outlets and shop online at
www.church-footwear.com/uk/en

* **58M:** Numerous brands of
shoes, an excellent selection.
57 rue Montmartre, 75002 Paris;
tel. +33 01 40 26 61 01
Shop online at www.58m.fr

* **K Jacques**
16 rue Pavée, 75004 Paris;
tel. +33 01 40 27 03 57
Shop online at www.kjacques.fr/en

SNEAKERS

* **Adidas**
3 rue des Rosiers, 75004 Paris;
tel. +33 01 53 01 93 60
Find retailers and shop online at
www.adidas.com/us

* **Converse**
Available at Citadium, 56 rue de
Caumartin, 75009 Paris
Find retailers and shop online at
www.converse.com

* **Golden Goose**
1 rue des Saints-Pères, 75006 Paris;
tel. +33 01 42 36 58 87
Find retailers at www.goldengoose
deluxebrand.com/us/en

HANDBAGS

* **Céline**
53 avenue Montaigne, 75008 Paris;
tel. +33 01 40 70 07 03
Find retailers at www.celine.com/en

* **Jérôme Dreyfuss**
1 rue Jacob, 75006 Paris;
tel. +33 01 43 54 70 93
Find retailers and shop online at
www.jerome-dreyfuss.com/fr_en

* **APC**
23 rue Royale, 75008 Paris;
tel. +33 01 44 51 98 57
Find retailers and shop online at
usonline.apc.fr

JEWELRY

* **Stone Paris:** The fine and
diamond-sprinkled jewelry of
my sister, Marie Poniatowski.
60 rue des Saints-Pères, 75006 Paris;
tel. +33 01 42 22 24 24
Find retailers at www.stoneparis.com
/en/news

* **Messika**
259 rue Saint-Honoré, 75001 Paris;
tel. +33 01 70 39 18 00
Find retailers at www.messika.com/en

* **Aurélie Bidermann**
55 bis rue des Saints-Pères, 75006
Paris; tel. +33 01 45 48 43 14
Find retailers and shop online at
www.aureliebidermann.com/edito/en

Kids' Rooms

Let's be clear, children are our marvels, our suns, our stars.
We want their rooms to be as fine as kingdoms.
But there can be a considerable chasm between their
questionable tastes (superheroes, mountains of stuffed animals)
and one's own desire for a modicum of chic.
So here's how to deal with it.

KEEPING THINGS TIDY

It's probably the main topic for a child's room. How do you keep things from spilling all over the place?

100 PERCENT NATURAL

To a child, "putting things away" means moving objects around or spreading the contents of a room all over the place. What's needed are containers, containers, and more containers. I ban all plastic. Why? Because it's usually ugly, and ugliness invites disorder. Also, it's not good for you, off-gassing harmful compounds, and children spend a lot of time in their rooms, even if they're only there at night. Once again (don't mess with a winning lineup), I advocate using natural materials: wood, wicker, bamboo, felt, metal. . . .

HAVE LOTS OF SMART STORAGE

★ Put yourself in the child's position. There's no point in having storage high off the ground for a five-year-old. Children under ten need lots of storage at ground level: little drawers under the bookcases, big rattan baskets with covers.

★ Make shelves for plush toys. Instead of letting them wind up in a heap on the bed or the floor, install a low shelf, about twelve inches (⅓ m) wide, where a child's security blankets and stuffed animals can be lined up on display.

★ Toss toys out from time to time. About every six months, sort through your child's things. What no longer interests her, what she's grown out of, goes into the giveaway pile for a charitable organization.

THE ART OF PLAY

The bedroom can be made a place for play.
Here are six ways.

A SWING

It's every child's secret dream. To install it, first make sure that the ceiling is strong enough, then invest in some solid wall anchors. The rest is a question of taste, though I personally recommend a vintage look: a thick rope + a wooden seat.

A CLIMBING ROPE

A variation on the swing, the climbing rope sometimes works better in a small room. Ideally? Install it in a corner, using a thick rope with knots every twenty inches. That way the child can climb AND swing.

A HAMMOCK

Do you have an exposed wall beam? Suspend a hammock from it for lounging in. You can also hang the hammock from the ceiling using two hooks (with four hooks you can hang a bed from the ceiling). I like natural artisan-made hammocks of woven cotton or canvas.

A BASKETBALL NET

Perfect for boys with too much energy. Install the hoop about six and a half feet off the floor for eight- to ten-year-olds. Protect the wall immediately behind it with a sturdy latex paint.

A DRAWING WALL

A simple idea, but it can be a big hit. Do your children love to draw on the walls? Let's give them a dedicated wall to do it on. Paint a section of wall with blackboard paint, ideally framing it with a band of color.

A PRACTICE BAR FOR DANCE

Perfect for all the little girls who dream of becoming ballerinas! Pair it with a large mirror, like in a real dance studio.

TREASURE TROVES FOR TOYS

★ **Si Tu Veux:** A little gem of a store tucked away in the galerie Vivienne, where you can find classic books and toys from the last fifty years.
68 galerie Vivienne, 75002 Paris; tel. +33 01 42 60 59 97; www.situveuxjouer.com

★ **Au Nain Bleu:** This is THE store for ultra-chic toys, incredible stuffed animals, old-fashioned dolls, puppets, and costumes.
252 boulevard Saint-Germain, 75007 Paris; tel. +33 01 42 65 20 00; boutique.aunainbleu.com

ENLIST THE CHILDREN IN DECORATING THEIR ROOMS

What if we bring the children into the decorating process? Within limits, their involvement can be positive. You just need to make a game of it!

PAINTING THE FLOOR

It's an excellent way of dealing with a less than pristine parquet floor, especially in a child's room. The best way is to lay down a solid primary coat, then a layer of very durable paint, the kind used for painting lines on asphalt. Paint stripes over certain sections of the floor, or over the entire floor.

PAINTING (PART OF) THE WALLS

A band of bright color (plum, deep purple, peacock blue, red) at the height of three feet above the base of the walls gives a child's room a distinctive touch. And it will camouflage the marks the child might make with his or her toys.

MAKE COLOR SPLOTCHES

Why not paint areas of color on a wall? Mark off a section, then distribute watercolors and paintbrushes, along with a few guidelines: round shapes, lines, and dots. Get to work!

BUY PRETTY FURNITURE

There's no need to skimp on style. Some children's furniture today is playful and at the same time handsome, sturdy, and practical. The child will be happy, and the parent too.

MY USEFUL ADDRESSES

★ **Petit Pan:** For their fabrics and their bamboo-and-silk animal trophies.
39 rue François-Miron, 75004 Paris; tel. +33 01 42 74 57 16; www.petitpan.com

★ **AM.PM.** products at www.laredoute.com

★ **Laurette**'s neo-retro furniture at www.laurette-deco.com/en

★ **The design collections** at en.smallable.com

★ **Les Enfants du Design:** Wonderful furniture and accessories (e.g., BudtzBendix chairs and fabric tents) at www.lesenfantsdudesign.com

★ And, of course, flea markets, swap meets, and websites for **secondhand goods**.

THE MINIMUM EQUIPMENT

With good crayons, pastels, felt-tip pens, etc., your children will undoubtedly make wonderful things. But the good news is that you don't need a great deal to have fun, especially when it comes to drawing. My recommendation is that thirty crayons and twelve felt-tips are enough to start with.

DRESS UP THEIR WALLS WITH DRAWINGS

The explosion of XXL coloring-book images is brilliant. When my son Roman was little, we put a big coloring-book drawing on his wall, and every night we filled in a part of it together before reading a story. It gave us a little ritual.

* Smart coloring-book pictures: Jungle Dudes color-in wallpaper
www.mrperswall.com

* Giant wall poster of Paris
www.omy.fr/shop/en/

* I Draw Laurent removable and reglueable color-in wallpaper
www.thecollection.fr/en

* XL color-in drawing of a town
Search for "coloriage géant" at www.hema.fr

HIGHLIGHT THEIR ARTWORK

I regularly collect my sons' best drawings— as I did for Yasmine when she was younger— and I have them framed in natural oak or black frames. Then I sprinkle them around pretty much everywhere—in their room, obviously, but also in my office and in the hallways. Some people take it further. Karine Sabolovic, for instance, an illustrator who founded madamepopandkids.fr, will touch up the children's drawings a little, and the images can then be transferred onto pillows, lamps, or coffee mugs.

CHILDREN AS ARTISTS

Inside each child slumbers a great artist. Let's help them express their creative potential! And let's preserve the best of their "works."

INTRODUCE THEM TO PHOTOGRAPHY

Children work very creatively with a camera. Their haphazard framing can prove to be poetic, as can their experiments with photo app filters. I sometimes preserve photographs of theirs by having them professionally printed, thanks to us.whitewall.com.

ARTIST WORKSHOPS

Children love to play with paint, crayons, and scissors. At my house on the weekends, we often have "wild workshops," where the children have fun making things, a little like their father. They paint with brushes or their fingers, they cut, they paste.... It always results in quite marvelous things. My technique? Lay down a tarp and give them free rein, dressed in old T-shirts and jeans.

KEEPING THEM BUSY: MUSEUMS, PARKS, AND TECHNOLOGY

Art is essential to the world, at least I think so. It shapes your mind, nourishes your imagination, opens your eyes to new perspectives, cultivates your capacity for tolerence.... In short, it promotes essential values. And I love it. So I take my children to see art exhibits all the time. Here are my top tips for museums and outdoor spaces to explore with your children, plus some apps for rainy days, or when you don't want to leave the house.

GOOD MUSEUMS

Most of them have hands-on workshops for children, often linked to their temporary exhibitions.

* **Musée du Louvre:** Right near our house. An amazing place.
75001 Paris; tel. +33 01 40 20 50 50
www.louvre.fr/en

* **Fondation Cartier:** Always a sure bet, and in a quiet neighborhood.
261 boulevard Raspail, 75014 Paris; tel. +33 01 42 18 56 50
www.fondation.cartier.com/#/en/home

* **Centre Pompidou:** The exhibits are top-notch, and the view of Paris priceless.
Place Georges-Pompidou, 75004 Paris; tel. +33 01 44 78 12 33
www.centrepompidou.fr/en

* **Jeu de Paume:** Also right near our house; they have great photo exhibits.
1 place de la Concorde, 75008 Paris; tel. +33 01 47 03 12 50
www.jeudepaume.org/index.php?lang=en

* **Maison Européenne de la Photographie:** For its thematic photo exhibitions.
5 rue de Fourcy, 75004 Paris; tel. +33 01 44 78 75 00
www.mep-fr.org/english

* **La Cité des Sciences:** A super space for children with an instructive permanent exhibition and a very large green space.
30 avenue Corentin-Cariou, 75019 Paris; tel. +33 01 40 05 80 00
www.lavillette.com/en

* **Musée d'Orsay:**
THE museum of the nineteenth century, in a former train station with classic architecture.
1 rue de la Légion d'Honneur, 75007 Paris; tel. +33 01 40 94 48 14
www.musee-orsay.fr/en/home.html

* **Musée Marmottan Monet:** A tiny museum, full of poetry, with magnificent Impressionist paintings.
2 rue Louis-Boilly, 75016 Paris; tel. +33 01 44 96 50 33
www.marmottan.fr/uk

* **Musée Jacquemart-André:** Nice exhibitions and a cozy tearoom for hot chocolate afterward.
158 boulevard Haussmann, 75008 Paris; tel. +33 01 45 62 11 59
www.musee-jacquemart-andre.com/en/home

* **Musée de la Vie Romantique:** A little gem of a museum, with a garden full of roses.
16 rue Chaptal, 75009 Paris; tel. +33 01 55 31 95 67
www.vie-romantique.paris.fr/en

* **Musée Rodin:** An introduction to the work of the great sculptor, in a town house set in a wonderful garden.
79 rue de Varenne, 75007 Paris; tel. +33 01 44 18 61 10
www.musee-rodin.fr/en

* **Cité de l'Architecture et du Patrimoine:** A little-known museum with superb reproductions of frescos, sculptures, architectural models...
1 place du Trocadéro, 75016 Paris; tel. +33 01 58 51 52 00
www.citechaillot.fr/en

* **La Grande Galerie de l'Évolution:** An astonishing place, with whale skeletons, taxidermied animals, and fascinating exhibitions.
36 rue Geoffroy-Saint-Hilaire, 75005 Paris; tel. +33 012 40 79 54 79
www.grandegaleriedelevolution.fr

* **Château de Versailles:** For its extra-large exhibits in the gardens, always by top-flight artists.

Place d'Armes, 78000 Versailles;
tel. +33 01 30 83 78 00
en.chateauversailles.fr

THE BEST PARKS

Children have to let off steam!

* **Jardin des Tuileries:** My children's playground since day one! 75001 Paris

* **Jardin du Luxembourg:** The big park on the Left Bank. On the down side, there are the many activities you have to pay for. 75006 Paris

* **Jardin du Palais-Royal:** An open enclave in the city, a place to kick a ball around. 75001 Paris

* **Le Jardin d'Acclimatation:** THE gathering place for young Parisians since forever!
Bois de Boulogne, 75016 Paris
www.jardindacclimatation.fr/pdf/GP_VMariotti_16.pdf

* **Parc de Bagatelle:** Exquisite in springtime, when all the roses are in bloom. 75016 Paris

* **Parc des Buttes-Chaumont:** Lovely views over Paris, a waterfall, architectural follies, and lawns where you can stretch out or play games! 75019 Paris

* **Jardin Anne Frank:** A small garden surrounded by handsome buildings. 75003 Paris

* **Parc André-Citroën:** An excellent park with beautiful lawns, a tethered hot-air balloon for viewing Paris from above, and jets of water in which to cool off. 75015 Paris

AND ALSO...

* **The FIAC:** Every year during the month of October. THE meeting place for lovers of contemporary art from around the world, where all the major galleries exhibit.
www.fiac.com/paris/en

* **Paris Photo:** Every November, a gathering of the best photography from all over the world. www.parisphoto.com

APPS FOR CHILDREN

* **Sago Mini Monsters:** A very amusing app for small children. They create monsters, feed them, and even have to brush their teeth.
Starting at eighteen to twenty-four months; www.sagosago.com/app/sago_mini_monsters

* **ShapeKit:** An intuitive app for creating art using shapes, colors, drawings, animations.
From three to four years;
kidkit.co/shapekit

* **The Robot Factory:** An incredible factory for building robots.
From five years;
tinybop.com/apps/the-robot-factory

* **Adobe Slate:** An app that makes it easy to create illustrated stories using photographs.
From six years;
standout.adobe.com/slate

* **Tinkerplay:** An app that introduces you to making figurines for 3-D printing.
From eight years;
www.123dapp.com/tinkerplay

Art at home: In my garden stands a sculpture by the artist Ben Swildens, given to me by my friends on my birthday. What better way to teach kids to get into art than to showcase it in your home!

DECORATING FOR TEENS

Adolescence is a period of transition and comes with its symbolic markers. Changing one's bedroom from a kid's room to a young adult's is an important one.

MIXING UP THE FURNITURE

There's nothing worse than a room with an overall look and matching furniture—bed, desk, wardrobe. They need to be unmatched to tip the look toward pre-adulthood. Again, the preference should be for natural materials.

THINK LOFT

An excellent way to set off the sleeping area from the working and living areas is to create a bed loft. It also makes the best use of a small space. For Yasmine, I made a tiny bed loft to "enlarge" her room and make it feel like a boat cabin.

MAKE THE BED BIGGER

After the tiny bed of childhood comes the transition to a bigger person's bed. Not so happy to see your child hop into a double bed that can sleep two people? Compromise with a twin, which takes up less room.

ENLARGE THE DESK

Young children work well on small desks, but adolescents often need more space for their computer, their notebooks, their objects. . . . Here too, you promote them to the next size up. One way is to support a surface of 47 × 31 inches (1.2 × .75 m) on two sawhorses. Another option is to use a secondhand table for the purpose.

STORAGE ALL AROUND

For big kids, I love installing a high shelf all the way around the room, just above the level of the doorframe. They can store all sorts of stuff on it without losing any space, and it gives the room structure.

RESPECT THEIR UNIVERSE

Are they crazy about horror films? Do they swoon over pop stars? OK. Bad taste goes away, or at least changes over the years. Removable and reusable adhesive is the best friend of parents who like pretty decorations!

MOTHER-DAUGHTER: THE COMMON WARDROBE

I don't know about you, but I share my wardrobe with my daughter, though not always of my own free will.

GIRLS AND THEIR MOTHERS' CLOSETS

I never really stole much from my mother's closet. It might have been a generational thing or a style thing. And my sister, Marie, who is two years older than me, always defended her stuff fiercely. With Yasmine, it's different. She has been rooting through my drawers for a long time now, borrowing just about everything, from clothes to shoes. We wear exactly the same sizes, from head to toe. Does it bother me? No. In fact, I'm happy to share my love for a particular fashion with her. It makes us closer. The one thing that bothers me? Seeing nice clothes of mine (which I may have been trying to find for months) being casually worn by one of her girlfriends!

DIFFERENT STYLES

Yasmine and I don't have the same style. I like a masculine-feminine style: shirts, jackets, sneakers. Yasmine has very idiosyncratic tastes. She picks up clothes at flea markets, raids vintage stores like Kilo Shop (69-71 rue de la Verrerie, 75004 Paris, and 125 boulevard Saint-Germain, 75006 Paris; www.kilo-shop.fr/en), or Kiliwatch (64 rue Tiquetonne, 75002 Paris; www.kiliwatch.fr/en). Her look is somewhat neo-eighties, along the lines of the schoolgirl Vic in Claude Pinoteau's La Boum. Yet she spent her childhood disguised as a princess, even when accompanying me to shop at Colette! So, there's no use in getting too anxious about these things. Her favorite stores are American Apparel (41 rue du Temple, 75004 Paris; tel. +33 01 42 74 71 03; store.americanapparel.net), Urban Outfitters (available at BHV Marais, 52 rue de Rivoli, 75004 Paris; tel. +33 09 77 40 14 00; www.urbanoutfitters.com), and, of course, Topshop (us.topshop.com).

WHAT THE DAUGHTER STEALS FROM HER MOTHER

My oxfords, especially a pair of pink ones from Jil Sander. Certain pairs of sneakers. My T-shirts, my sweaters, my pants . . . Where do I draw the line? The beautiful and very chic items are off-limits! Sometimes I even give her the clothes that she particularly loves, or I make a present of them on big occasions—Christmas and birthdays.

GOOD MANNERS

Good manners are as indispensable as oxygen! I'm relaxed about many things, but I hold the line at manners. At my mother's house, the rules were the rules. And one of my grandmothers was extremely strict: With her, no way were you going to play it cool! We ate in the kitchen, we came into the drawing room to say hello to the adults, we spoke only when addressed. Sometimes when I see my children, I think our educations have left a chasm between us!

POLITENESS

"Good morning" is a proof of civility right at the start of the day. I expect it, along with a kiss, every morning. Same for "good night." "Thank you" is not negotiable. Nor is "please."

KINDNESS

I value kindness very highly, because I think it makes the world more livable. All three of my children are deeply kind by nature. But I've always also tried to cultivate the habit in them.

RESPECT FOR OTHERS

Another fundamental value. If children want to be respected as individuals, they need to learn to respect the wishes, desires, and activities of others. And that extends to me as well, especially when I want to take a quiet bath!

SHARING

We live in a family and belong also to a larger community of friends and social acquaintances. We must each learn to share with others: our time, space, attention, possessions....

SCREENS

A big issue. And it's hard to imagine how a smartphone maniac like me is going to limit the children's access to screens. In the country, I push everyone out of the house as early as possible! It's better for them to be playing outside. In Paris, they are allotted a certain amount of screen time each day. It's up to them to manage it.

AUTONOMY

I adore my children, but I am even happier to see them grow up and become independent. I never wanted to keep them as babies by my side. I try, as they mature, to help them become independent in their daily lives.

RESPONSIBILITY

Another fundamental value. All our actions have positive or negative consequences. That's something that we can and must understand from childhood on. Am I strict? No, but I am their mother. Not their buddy.

Balcony, Terrace, *or* Garden

I don't have a green thumb at all, but I love the poetry of gardens, terraces, balconies. It doesn't take much space for nature to flourish.

MY GARDENING SECRETS

GIVE NATURE ROOM

I like it when a lawn is not too closely cropped. I always leave untamed areas where wild grasses and flowers can grow freely, for instance, around the bases of fruit trees. I often mow in strips, sometimes crosshatches.

LOTS OF FRUIT-BEARING PLANTS

They're beautiful, producing spectacular flowers in spring and fruits in summer. The cherry tree fruits in May, the raspberry bushes in June, and the fig tree at the end of summer. The idea is to always have fruits to pick in the garden.

SOW FLOWERS

In spring, you can spread the seeds of annual flowers (poppies, cornflowers, daisies) over grassy areas that you then leave unmown. It's pretty and looks rural.

PLANT ROSES, ETC.

I'm crazy about flowers and their scents. I like to see tons of rosebushes, especially climbing ones, in a garden; white and blue agapanthus in pots and in the ground; hydrangeas of all colors; star jasmine, which reminds me of Morocco....

ADVICE FOR THE TERRACE FROM LOUIS BENECH

Because I don't garden at all, I take advice from the pros. Louis Benech is a family friend. I remember vacationing with him as a child in the Arcachon Basin. Since those days, he has become a star: the Tuileries gardens, the Élysée gardens, Chaumont-sur-Loire, and the new Bosquet du Théâtre d'Eau at Versailles—that's all him! Here are his tips and tricks for making a terrace garden in the city.

Making a terrace garden

INSPECT THE SITE

Before launching into a terrace (or balcony) project, you must take accurate stock of the site, answering a number of very specific questions:

* In which direction does the terrace face?

* Do other buildings loom overhead?

* How much sunlight does the terrace get?

* Is there much wind?

* What are the sight lines?

CALCULATE THE WEIGHT

Wet earth can be very heavy. On a planted terrace, the weight can reach several tons, while the load limit is generally around 30 pounds per square foot (150 kilograms per square meter). If the terrace is not strong enough, cracks will develop. And the owner of the terrace will be responsible for any damage. It's therefore important to reduce the weight as much as possible.
* Replace clay pots with pots made of fiber or moss-lined mesh.

* Lighten the potting soil by mixing it with expanded clay pellets, which are necessary for drainage, and with Misapor, a foam glass gravel that lowers the soil's weight while fostering root growth. Info at www.misapor.ch/EN/Home.html.

CHECK FOR WATERPROOFNESS

If there are cracks, even tiny ones, water will infiltrate them. This is a given. Before installing your terrace garden, have a specialist check that the surface is watertight. Even then, it's best to plant in tubs that rest on rollers, which are easy to move in case of a leak.

AVOID KNOWN MISFITS

Some plants are entirely wrong for a terrace, including bamboo, birch, and willow. Why? Because these plants love water and their powerful roots can penetrate everywhere. They can even pierce through an irrigation hose and "sense" the presence of water from the condensation on a pipe's surface. There is just one solution: Avoid them entirely.

MAKE YOUR LIFE EASIER

Urban terraces are often exposed to high winds and dry very quickly. You can install an automatic watering system, but it brings with it the dangers of leaks and flooding. Another option is to choose drought-resistant plants that will need little or no watering. A cactus garden would fit the bill, or plants native to dry regions.

A minimalist concept or a pretty tangle of greenery?

BENECH'S RECOMMENDED PLANTS

Coastal grasses

Native to a seaside environment, they are adapted to harsh conditions (wind, salt). European beachgrass (*Ammophila arenaria*) and sand ryegrass (*Leymus arenarius*) are perfect for our terraces.

Laurustinus

Or *Viburnum tinus*. This shrub grows to a maximum height of 10 feet (3 m), its leaves are evergreen, and it flowers in winter, from November to March. It is hardy and grows in both shade and sunlight.

Rosebushes

Naturally. Among the varieties that are current favorites: Pierre de Ronsard, the striped climbing rose École de Barbizon, Briosa, Comte de Chambord.

Star jasmine

Or *Trachelospermum jasminoides*. A wonderful climbing plant, it flowers in late spring and has a delicious scent. It also keeps its foliage through the winter and requires little maintenance other than some water.

Lavenders

There are more than twenty-eight species of lavender, all of them hardy, sun tolerant, cold resistant, and drought resistant. Their enemy? Too much water. Putting lavender on a balcony or terrace is a sure way to invite bees to visit.

A FIVE-MINUTE BOUQUET

A few flowers and a vase or a bottle are all it takes to bring a touch
of poetry to the house.

GOOD MIXTURES
In the center, lovely sweet-smelling
blossoms, mixed with wild grasses,
surrounded by leaves and branches in
the spring.

VASES
All sorts of things can be pressed into use
as vases: big candleholders, canning jars,
large glasses, carafes. . . .

TYING THEM IN A BUNCH
I prefer to use the most natural materials
possible. My favorites? Raffia, sisal twine, a
cotton ribbon. These also look very decorative around an improvised vase.

FLOWER ARRANGEMENT

For an eye-catching bouquet on a small budget: Cut the flowers to the height of the vase and group them in "color spots" without mixing; it's much more modern. A good mixture might be roses, the green foliage of raspberry or mulberry, and white carnations. Or peonies, lavender, and ivy. For an even greater effect, I make bouquets in old-fashioned silver tumblers or in lowball glasses and put them on the table next to the sofa. I also just use glass bottles in different sizes and group them together with a flower in each, a little like Tsé & Tsé's April Vase, but homemade.

HAVE A PICNIC!

I set up a table at the bottom of my garden, and children and adults all flock to it. We plunk ourselves down any which way, then take a siesta on the grass.

THE TABLE

The ideal is to have a "table" resting on legs about sixteen to twenty inches (40 to 50 cm) high. This lets you eat off a solid surface while sitting on the ground. Otherwise, a nice tartan rug or a tablecloth spread on the grass will do the trick. All around, I set masses of assorted cushions for seating, laying them on rugs. For dinnerware, I love using the enameled metal plates from Merci (111 boulevard Beaumarchais, 75011 Paris; www.merci-merci.com/en). The children drink out of melamine cups from Rice (www.rice. dk/en-us). I add some pretty cloth or paper napkins, a few bouquets of wild flowers, and we're good to go!

MY RECIPES FOR DINING AL FRESCO

For 4 to 6 people.

Vegetable gratin

In an oiled baking dish, set alternating slices of zucchini, eggplant, tomato, and onion upright next to each other. The slices should be ¼ inch (5 mm) thick. Drizzle olive oil over the tightly packed whole. Sprinkle thyme over it, and salt and pepper. Cook for 2 to 3 hours at 300°F (150°C). Let it cool somewhat and reheat before serving.

Roasted peppers

On a baking sheet lined with parchment paper, place 10 red bell peppers, washed and split lengthwise, with their stems and seeds removed. Set them in an oven heated to 350°F (180°C) for 20 to 30 minutes. When the skins start to blacken, remove and seal them in a plastic bag. Let them cool for an hour. Peel them and wipe them with a paper towel. Arrange the peppers on a serving plate, drizzle olive oil on them, and sprinkle with minced garlic, salt, and pepper.

Strawberry-cherry compote

In a skillet, sauté 1 pound (500 g) of pitted black cherries in 1 tablespoon (14 g) of salted butter for 5 to 6 minutes, along with 1 vanilla pod, split lengthwise, and 2 heaping tablespoons (60 g) of sugar. Add 8 ounces (200 g) of strawberries and cook for another 2 minutes. Let it cool for half an hour, remove the vanilla pod, and serve with scoops of vanilla ice cream.

Lemonade

In a food processor, mix together 2 whole organic lemons (seeds removed) with a scant 2 tablespoons (60 g) of sugar. Pour the mixture into a sieve. Place the sieve over a funnel, and the funnel in the neck of a bottle. Pour in 3 cups (700 ml) of cold water. The lemony water becomes white. Leave it in the refrigerator for 1 hour before serving.

Melon-mozzarella salad

On a serving dish, place slices of cantaloupe and mozzarella di bufala. Add salt, pepper, a little basil, and a dash of olive oil.

Yellow gazpacho

In a food processor, put 3 pounds (1.5 kg) of yellow tomatoes with a splash of sherry vinegar, a little bread (without the crust), salt, pepper, and olive oil. Add a bit of very cold water. Blend them all together well and serve very cold.

String bean salad with peaches

Tip and tail 1 pound (500 g) of string beans and cook for 5 minutes in salted boiling water. Drain and rinse them quickly with cold water to preserve their color. Julienne 2 white peaches. In a serving dish, make a vinaigrette using 4 tablespoons (60 ml) of olive oil, 2 tablespoons (30 ml) of good sherry vinegar, salt, and pepper. Add the green beans and the peaches, toss them gently together, and top with a little minced basil.

Lime and mango ceviche

Cut a pound of seabream into ¼-inch (5 cm) pieces. Mix in a serving dish with the juice and zest of 2 limes. Cover and allow to marinate in the refrigerator for 6 hours. Add 2 chopped scallions, half a mango cut into small dice, 4 tablespoons (60 ml) of olive oil, and 2 tablespoons of chopped cilantro (coriander). Serve cold.

Asparagus, zucchini, and green pea quiche

Line a tart pan with puff pastry. Add ¼ pound (200 g) of fresh peas, 12 asparagus tips, and a zucchini cut lengthwise on a mandoline. Mix together 5 eggs, ½ cup (100 g) of crème fraîche, and salt and pepper, and add the mixture to the tart pan. Cook for 40 minutes at 350°F (180°C). Serve with a green salad.

Quinoa with lemon confit

Rinse 1 cup (200 g) of quinoa in several changes of water. Simmer for 20 minutes in 2 cups (475 ml) of water. Take it off the heat and let it sit covered. Stir with a fork and allow to cool. In a salad bowl, mix 2 confit lemons, chopped and deseeded; 3 slivered scallions; and 2 sprigs of chopped Italian parsley. Add the quinoa and mix together. Season with salt, pepper, olive oil, and lemon juice.

Veal roast with herb sauce

Cook a 3-pound (1.5 kg) veal roast in the oven at 350°F (180°C) for 45 minutes. Let it cool, then cut it into thin slices. Cover and refrigerate. In a serving dish, make mayonnaise using 1 egg white, 1 teaspoon (5 ml) strong Dijon mustard, salt, pepper, and 1 scant cup (200 ml) of sunflower oil. Add 4 ounces (100 g) of farmer's cheese, 1 tablespoon (15 ml) of lemon juice, 1 tablespoon (15 ml) each of chopped Italian parsley, tarragon, chervil, and chives, and 1 teaspoon of chopped basil. Serve the herb sauce with the veal roast.

Roofs and chimney pots

Zinc sheets as far as the eye can see, that's my favorite view of Paris!
I've always chosen apartments just under the eaves, so that I
would have that view.

I need air, light, beauty.... In Paris, the
best place to enjoy them is all the way
up, on the roof, next to the chimney
pots. In each of my apartments, I've
always found a way to get onto the roof,
onto the zinc. My children sometimes
follow suit, even decorating the roof.
Why do I find it so appealing? It's like
the sea. The colors change according to
the time of day, the sun's position, the
weather. It must reflect my Peter Pan
syndrome. Since I can't go on being a
child and fly, I dream!

STAYING COOL!

TO SIESTA OR NOT TO SIESTA

In the country, I'm always busy; I don't have time for a nap. And though I don't fall asleep, I do like to read in the garden in the shade of a tree or on my terrace in the sun. The last books I really loved? *The Age of Reinvention*, by Karine Tuil; *Just Kids*, by Patti Smith; *Out of Africa*, by Karen Blixen; *Le Journal d'un corps*, by Daniel Pennac; and *The Power of Now*, by Eckhart Tolle.

LET'S HEAR IT FOR SPORTS!

With two sons ages eight and five, I naturally spend lots of time running around. When we're in the garden we're normally playing: soccer, volleyball, badminton, any game that

uses a ball or a projectile! A second option when it's hot is to play with the garden hose. We spend hours chasing each other with the spray nozzle. Lots of laughing and giggling. I regress to the point where I'm barely ten years old myself.

ART

I've already said that I'm nuts about contemporary art. I've even managed to install a piece in my garden. How? Thanks to my friends who pitched in to give me a magnificent sculpture by Ben Swildens for my fortieth birthday. It has a place of honor in our garden. I sometimes meditate in front of it or climb it like a kid.

My useful addresses

FLORISTS

* Vert et Plus
14 rue Saint-Roch, 75001 Paris;
tel. +33 01 40 20 42 80

* Moulié Fleurs
8 place du Palais-Bourbon, 75007
Paris; tel. +33 01 45 51 78 43
mouliefleurs.com/english

* Roses Costes Dani Roses
Hôtel Costes, 239 rue Saint-Honoré,
75001 Paris; tel. +33 01 42 44 50 09
hotelcostes.com/#/en/costes/
54/life-at-costes/63
/roses-costes-dani-roses

* Sylvine
98 rue Beaubourg, 75003 Paris;
tel. +33 01 42 71 31 35

* Hervé Châtelain
140 rue Montmartre, 75002 Paris;
tel. +33 01 45 08 85 57

* Debeaulieu
30 rue Henri-Monnier, 75009 Paris;
tel. +33 0145 26 78 68
www.debeaulieu-paris.com

* Muse
4 rue Burq, 75018 Paris;
tel. +33 01 46 06 52 49
www.muse-montmartre.fr

* Un Jour de Fleurs
Le Jardin, 22 rue Jean-Nicot, 75007
Paris; tel. +33 01 45 50 43 54

L'Atelier, 85 avenue du Roule,
92200 Neuilly-sur-Seine;
tel. +33 01 47 47 54 51

Le Marché, 77 avenue du Roule,
92200 Neuilly-sur-Seine;
tel. +33 01 47 22 55 67

www.ericchauvin.fr/en

* Atelier Marie-Marianne
6 rue du Général-Bertrand, 75015
Paris; tel. +33 01 44 49 01 05
www.mariemarianne.fr

* Odorantes
9 rue Madame, 75006 Paris;
tel. +33 01 42 84 03 00

* Au Jardin de Matisse
4 avenue Percier, 75008 Paris;
tel. +33 01 56 59 90 54
www.jardindematisse.com

GARDEN SUPPLIES AND NURSERIES

* CasaNova
10 quai de la Mégisserie, 75001 Paris;
tel. +33 01 53 60 18 43

* Marché aux fleurs et aux oiseaux: A charming
flower market close to the
Conciergerie.
Quai de la Corse, 75004 Paris

* Les Fermes de Gally
D7 route de Bailly, 78210 Saint-Cyr-
L'École; tel. +33 01 30 14 60 60
www.ferme.gally.com

* La Jardinerie de Chevreuse
87 route de Rambouillet, Ferme
du Breuil, 78460 Chevreuse;
tel. +33 01 30 52 28 32
jardinerie-chevreuse.fr

* Jardinerie Poullain
1 avenue des Platanes, 78940
La-Queue-les-Yvelines;
tel. +33 01 34 86 42 99
www.jardinerie-pepiniere-poullain.fr

* Jardinerie de la Jonchère
53 avenue de la Jonchère, 78170 La
Celle-Saint-Cloud; tel. +33 01 30 82 01 16
www.jardinerie-jonchere.fr

* Jardinerie Delbard Taverny
1–3 avenue Théodore-Monod, 95150
Taverny; tel. +33 01 34 18 60 81
www.delbard.fr

* Les Serres de Maubuisson
6 rue Alexandre-Prachay, 95310 Saint-
Ouen-l'Aumône; tel. +33 01 34 64 14 30
www.serres-de-maubuisson.com

LANDSCAPE DESIGNER

* Pierre-Alexandre Risser
5 sente des Fréculs, 95390 Saint-Prix-
Vieux-Village; tel. +33 01 34 27 90 19;
www.horticultureetjardins.com/
english-presentation

OUTDOOR FURNITURE

* Unopiù
58 place du Marché-Saint-Honoré,
75001 Paris; tel. +33 01 55 35 00 42
www.unopiu.com

* Le Cèdre Rouge
22 avenue Victoria, 75001 Paris;
tel. +33 01 42 33 71 05

La Briqueterie, RD 307, 78810
Feucherolles; tel. +33 01 76 78 36 20

www.lecedrerouge.com

* Fermob
81-83 avenue Ledru-Rollin, 75012
Paris; tel. +33 01 43 07 17 15
www.paris.fermob.com

* Tolix
Find retail locations at www.tolix.fr/en

* Dedon
40 boulevard Malesherbes, 75008
Paris; tel. +33 01 40 98 02 03

Find retail locations at
www.dedon.de/en

Traveling, Traveling

Bali, Tokyo, New York, Marrakech... Here are
my favorite addresses, my secrets from far away.
This is where I go to recharge. These are the
destinations that fill me with inspiration.

MARRAKECH FOREVER

Just a short hop from France. Three hours from Paris and you're in a completely different world. It's a special place for me, because I've been traveling there with my father since forever.

WHEN TO GO?

Any time of year is good except July and August, when it's sweltering.

MY HOTELS

* **Ksar Char-Bagh:** A sumptuous Relais & Châteaux hotel with Moorish architecture. Lovely garden, thoughtful service.
Djnan Abiad, La Palmeraie;
tel. +212 524 32 92 44
www.ksarcharbagh.com/?lang=en

* **Les Cinq Djellabas:** A very appealing boutique hotel in the Palmeraie decorated in a modern style.
Douar al Gribate, La Palmeraie;
tel. +212 644 091 091
www.hotel-les5djellabas.com

* **L'Amanjena:** A peaceful haven where I love going for lunch, then lazing by the pool. We often send our friends here.
Route de Ouarzazate, km 12;
tel. +212 524 399 000
www.amanresorts.com/amanjena

* **Mamounia Hotel:** It has to be seen for the beauty of its gardens, its idyllic décor, and its views of the Atlas Mountains.
Avenue Bab Jdid;
tel. +212 524 388 600
www.mamounia.com/en/marrakech.htm

MY RESTAURANTS

* **Cour des Lions:** A fine restaurant on the top floor of the Es Saadi Palace, right in the middle of Marrakech, in a superb setting created by the best local artisans. The food is by a student of the Pourcel brothers, Sébastien Bontour, who creatively revisits traditional Moroccan cuisine.
Es Saadi Palace, Rue Ibrahim El Mazini; tel. +212 663 581 599
www.essaadi.com/en/restaurants/the-palace-restaurants

* **Le Foundouk:** A very contemporary restaurant in an ancient *riad* (traditional Moroccan house). Excellent cuisine, half French and half Moroccan.
55 Souk Al Fassi, Kat Bennahïd;
tel. +212 524 378 176
www.foundouk.com/?langue=en

* **Jack Is Back:** This restaurant belongs to my friend Jacky Fourny. A relaxed atmosphere, delicious pizzas, and fun décor.
Boulevard Oued Al Makhazine;
tel. +212 524 433 890

* **Bô & Zin:** A festive place where the atmosphere and the music are always good. Fusion cooking.
Douar Lahna, route de l'Ourika, km 3.5;
tel. +212 524 388 012
www.bo-zin.com/en

MY SHOPS

* **Chez Zoé:** My favorite bed linens. Sheets, terry-cloth bathrobes, children's pajamas, women's djellabas—refinement in its purest state.
277 Zone Industrielle Sidi Ghanem; tel. +212 524 336 144
www.chezzoe.com

* **Moon Garden:** For sensible outdoor furniture.
310 Sidi Ghanem; tel. +212 524 335 588
www.moon-garden.com

* **Antiquités Moulay Youssef:** Moulay specializes in furniture and design of the 1950s to 1970s. A trove of eye-catching pieces!
On the road to Targa; Quartier Victor-Hugo

* **Bab el Khemis flea market:** Two dealers in particular: Abdessadk (stall No. 109) for antique furniture and accessories, and Adil (No. 136) for furniture and objects from the 1950s.

* **Ministero del Gusto:** A design studio with a showroom presenting furniture, jewelry, and vintage-style pieces.
22 derb Azzouz, el Mouassine; tel. +212 524 426 455
www.ministerodelgusto.com

* **Amira Bougies:** A very large selection of lovely paraffin candles.
277 Sidi Ghanem; tel. +212 524 336 117

* **Yahya Création:** A talented decorator and brassworker, Yahya Rouach, creates magnificent light fixtures in wood, iron, and copper.
61 rue Yougoslavie; tel. +212 524 422 776
www.yahya-group.com

* **Atelier Beldine:** A ceramics studio where the tableware is painted by the members of a women's collaborative.
Tamesloht; tel. +212 663 709 005
www.facebook.com/Beldine.atelier/

* **Scènes de Lin:** For its beautiful fabrics, its napkins, its embroidered cushions . . .
70 rue de la Liberté; tel. +212 524 436 108
www.scenesdelin.com

* **Mustapha Blaoui:** A shop tucked away in the medina that is full of old pieces and quality craftsmanship. Flasks, mirrors, fabrics, small pieces of furniture, tea sets, lamps—it has everything!
142–144 rue Bab Doukkala
www.mustaphablaoui.com

* **Kim & Garo:** Its cushions, its plaid blankets, and its traditional cotton-on-linen embroideries are superb.
Lot No. 42, Zone Industrielle de Tamesloht; tel. +212 524 483 068
www.kimetgaro.com/?lang=en

THE SOUKS OF MARRAKECH

In the heart of the medina, there lies a labyrinth where you look for treasures and get properly lost.

MY FAVORITE OUTING

* **The Jardin Majorelle** (rue Yves-Saint-Laurent) For its luxuriant vegetation and its unbelievable blue. And right next door, don't miss the concept store 33 rue Majorelle (33 rue Yves-Saint-Laurent), a kind of local mini-Colette. Everything there is nice, plus it has an excellent juice bar.
jardinmajorelle.com/ang

NEW YORK EXPRESS

I generally visit two or three times a year, a little oftener now that Barneys is carrying my line. I feel at home there. I already drive myself at a hundred miles an hour in Paris, but it's twice as bad in New York, and the vibe is so positive. In New York, everything is allowed; everything is possible!

WHEN TO GO?

Spring and fall are pleasant seasons in New York. In summer it gets very hot. And winters can be brutal!

MY HOTELS

* **The Mercer:** It never goes out of fashion! Its service and subdued style make it feel like home, but with all the elegance of Christian Liaigre furniture.
147 Mercer Street; tel. 212 966 6060
www.mercerhotel.com

* **The Crosby Street Hotel:** I already loved the Firmdale hotels in London. The decoration can be a little much, but in this hotel I like the large picture windows with their spectacular views.
79 Crosby Street; tel. 212 226 6400
www.firmdalehotels.com/hotels
/new-york/crosby-street-hotel

* **The Standard High Line:** In spring, you have to reserve a corner room for the magical view over the Hudson and the sunsets, visible from the bathtub. One downside: the nonexistent lobby.
848 Washington Street;
tel. 212 645 4646
www.standardhotels.com/new-york
/properties/high-line

* **The Mark:** On the Upper East Side, this handsome hotel near Central Park is ideal for early morning walks when badly jet-lagged. Cooking is by Jean-Georges. Classically styled by Jacques Grange.
25 E. 77th Street; tel. 212 744 4300
www.themarkhotel.com

* **The Bowery Hotel:** It's worth getting a room with a terrace on one of the upper floors. Hip. Different. Fun. Between Little Italy and Chinatown.
335 Bowery; tel. 212 505 9100
www.theboweryhotel.com

MY RESTAURANTS

* **The Mercer Kitchen:** I make the pilgrimage to sample its amazing truffle pizza!
99 Prince Street; tel. 212 966 5454
www.themercerkitchen.com

* **Eataly:** A fantastic, giant Italian-style grocery where you can also get a quick and delicious bite of lunch.
200 Fifth Avenue; tel. 212 229 2560
www.eataly.com/us_en/stores
/new-york

* **Colicchio & Sons:** An Italian restaurant in the Chelsea district with attentive service and wonderful food.
85 Tenth Avenue; tel. 212 400 6699
www.craftrestaurantsinc.com
/colicchio-and-sons

* **Nobu:** A classic. So frustrating not to have one in Paris.
105 Hudson Street; tel. 212 219 0500
www.noburestaurants.com/new-york
/experience

* **ABC Kitchen:** For its organic menu, almost entirely devoted to vegetables.
35 East 18th Street; tel. 212 475 5829
www.abchome.com/eat/abc-kitchen

* **Omen Azen:** New and fantastic Japanese!
113 Thompson Street;
tel. 212 925 8923
www.omen-azen.com

Blue Ribbon Sushi: A good place to sample excellent sushi prepared by a master.
119 Sullivan Street; tel. 212 343 0404
www.blueribbonrestaurants.com
/restaurants/blue-ribbon-sushi-original

Sant Ambroeus: The setting is amazing and the pasta to die for! An important landmark for a pasta addict like me.
259 West 4th Street; tel. 212 604 9254
www.santambroeus.com/sa_west
_village.html

La Esquina: An excellent restaurant serving true and delicious Mexican cuisine.
114 Kenmare Street; tel. 646 613 7100
www.esquinanyc.com

The Boom Boom Room: A fantastic 360-degree view of the city from the rooftop, particularly magical at sunset.
The Standard High Line,
848 Washington Street;
tel. 212 645 4646
www.standardhotels.com

Balthazar: For a nice little lunch in a French enclave in the heart of the Big Apple.
80 Spring Street; tel. 212 965 1414
www.balthazarny.com

The Ides Bar: The bar in the Wythe Hotel in Brooklyn, with an incredible view of New York's skyline.
80 Wythe Avenue; tel. 718 460 8000
www.wythehotel.com/the-ides

MY SHOPS

ABC Carpet & Home: An interior decorating store with modern rugs and designer furniture.
888 + 881 Broadway;
tel. 212 473 3000
www.abchome.com

Ralph Pucci International: Part gallery, part furniture and design store; a unique establishment where they sell unique pieces.
44 W. 18th Street; tel. 212 633 0452
www.ralphpucci.net

Alexander Wang: For his great T-shirts!
103 Grand Street; tel. 212 977 9683
www.alexanderwang.com

James Perse: Here too the T-shirts are superb, in ultra-soft cotton and very comfortable.
60 Mercer Street; tel. 212 334 3501
www.jamesperse.com

Anthropologie: An all-in-one store carrying women's fashion, accessories, designer objects...
Chelsea Market, 75 Ninth Avenue (plus other locations); tel. 212 620 3116
www.anthropologie.com

Ralph Lauren RRL: For his vintage bomber jackets, his sweaters, his beautifully finished shirts.
31 Prince Street; tel. 212 343 0841
www.ralphlauren.com

What Goes Around Comes Around: One of the best vintage clothing stores in New York.
351 West Broadway; tel. 212 343 1225
www.whatgoesaroundnyc.com

Kirna Zabête: A concept store with a truly excellent selection of fashions, from Rykiel to Jason Wu, via Anthony Vaccarello and Chloé.
477 Broome Street; tel. 212 941 9656
www.kirnazabete.com

* **McNally Jackson Books:**
One of my favorite bookstores, with more than 55,000 books!
52 Prince Street; tel. 212 274 1160
www.mcnallyjackson.com

Roll & Hill: A great store for ultra-contemporary light fixtures.
32 33rd Street, Unit 10
Brooklyn, NY; tel. 718 387 6132
www.rollandhill.com

* **Lindsey Adelman Studio:**
Another good location for fans of poetic light fixtures and beautiful objects.
tel. 212 473 2501
www.lindseyadelman.com

MY GALLERIES

R & Company: A gallery with a fine selection of vintage furniture, light fixtures, and designer objects, since 1997.
82 Franklin Street; tel. 212 343 7979
www.r-and-company.com

Cristina Grajales Gallery: A gallery that combines twentieth-century furniture and the light fixtures of the future.
152 W. 25th Street, 3rd Floor;
tel. 212 219 9941
www.cristinagrajalesinc.com

* **Johnson Trading Gallery:**
Contemporary art, architecture, and design.
47-42 43rd Street, Woodside, NY 11377; tel. 212 925 1110
www.johnsontradinggallery.com

* **Gagosian Gallery:** One of the great contemporary art galleries anywhere in the world. There's always something there to discover.
555 W. 24th Street; tel. 212 741 1111
www.gagosian.com

* **David Zwirner Gallery:** A gallery representing more than forty artists, among them Yayoi Kusama, Richard Serra, and Jeff Koons.
525 W. 19th Street; tel. 212 727 2070
www.davidzwirner.com

* **Brooklyn Flea:** The market has about a hundred stalls, and there's always something of interest if you're willing to dig for it. Find locations at www.brooklynflea.com

MY OUTINGS

* The Egyptian rooms at **The Metropolitan Museum of Art** for the collection and the view of Central Park. 1000 Fifth Avenue; www.metmuseum.org

* The new **Whitney Museum of American Art** A Renzo Piano design. 99 Gansevoort Street; www.whitney.org

* **American Museum of Natural History** Perfect for an outing with the children. Central Park West and 79th Street; www.amnh.org

* **The Museum of Modern Art** Of course . . .
11 W. 53rd Street; www.moma.org

* And finally, the **High Line**, which I follow uptown to the galleries in Chelsea. The public park runs along a former elevated freight rail line from Gansevoort Street to West 34th Street, between 10th and 12th Avenues

BALI ZEN

I've summered there many times in the month of August. It is a top-notch destination for children, because everyone is super nice, the climate is mild, and the sea is warm.

WHEN TO VISIT?

From April to October, when the weather is cooler and less humid.

MY HOTELS

* **The Legian:** A large hotel with low-key décor, next to a long beach of white sand.
Jalan Kayu Aya, Seminyak Beach;
tel. +62 361 730 622
lhm-hotels.com/legian-bali/en

* **Amankila:** A sumptuous resort on the island's southeast coast between the mountains, the forest, and the sea. Split-level swimming pools, fabulous décor . . .
Manggis; tel. +62 363 41 333
www.aman.com/resorts/amankila

* **Uma by COMO, Ubud:** Almost certainly the finest hotel in Ubud, a small town in Bali's uplands.
Jalan Raya Sanggingan, Banjar Lungsiakan, Kedewatan, Ubud;
tel. +62 361 972 448
www.comohotels.com/umaubud

* **Alila Villas Uluwatu:** A set of villas with private pools, plus a fifty-meter swimming pool, twenty-four-hour reception desk, a spa, a library . . . Home, but at the hotel!
Jalan Belimbing Sari, Banjar, Tambiyak, Desa Pecatu, Uluwatu;
tel. +62 361 848 2166
www.alilahotels.com/uluwatu

MY RESTAURANTS

* **Sardine:** An open-air restaurant run by a French chef, where you dine under a bamboo roof, with a view over rice paddies.
Jalan Petitenget 21, Kerobokan;
tel. +62 811 397 8111
www.sardinebali.com

* **Watercress Bali:** From breakfast to dinner, the menu is organic and vegetarian, the portions generous, the food delicious.
Jolan Batu Belig 21a, Kerobokan;
tel. +62 361 780 8030
www.watercressbali.com

* **Métis:** A place to enjoy Mediterranean cooking while looking out at the Balinese landscape. Superb décor.
Jalan Petintenget 6, Kerobokan;
tel. +62 361 4731 456
www.metisbali.com

* **Mama San:** An indoor restaurant (rare in Bali) with the restaurant on one floor, and a bar and a cooking school upstairs. Vintage décor and Asiatic cooking.
Jalan Raya, Kerobokan 135, Banjar Taman, Kuta; tel. +62 361 730 436
www.mamasanbali.com

* **Urchin Grill & Raw Bar:** Innovative seafood in an elegant, low-key setting.
Badung Regency, Kuta;
tel. +62 361 736 319
www.urchinbali.com

MY SHOPS

* **Casamayor:** An interior decorating store with small objects, candles, and sculpture.
Jalan Pantai Berawa, Canggu;
tel. +62 818 0540 0115
www.casamayorbali.com

* **Gaya Ceramic and Design:** In Ubud, a workshop that makes stoneware, porcelain, and raku for the palaces of Bali and for export.
Jalan Raya Sayan, Ubud;
tel. +62 361 976 220
www.gayaceramic.com

* **Étienne de Souza:** A lovely design firm run by a Frenchman who makes contemporary inlaid furniture, screens . . .
Seminyak; tel. +62 361 730 942
www.etiennedesouza.com

TOKYO SPIRIT

A wonderful destination, and I'm lucky enough to go there from time to time! It's completely different from the West; there, the design movement is very strong, and there still exists a genuine crafts culture.

WHEN TO VISIT?

In spring or fall. Summers can be hot and very humid, winters on the cold side but pleasant.

MY HOTELS

* **Park Hyatt Tokyo:** In Shinjuku, with large, noise-insulated rooms and thoughtful service. Also? A very *Lost in Translation* ambience!
3-7-1-2 Nishi Shinjuku, Shinjuku-ku;
tel. +81 3 5322 1234
www.tokyo.park.hyatt.com

* **Hotel Okura:** One of the best-known hotels in Tokyo because of its 1960s modernist architecture. Unfortunately, the main building is closed for renovations until 2019. But the south wing is still open.
2-10-4 Toranomon Minato-ku;
tel. +81 3 3582 0111
www.hotelokura.co.jp/tokyo/en

MY RESTAURANTS

* **Takazawa:** A restaurant I ADORED, the next El Bulli, sure to be named "the world's best restaurant" next year. An amazing experience (eight courses), but horribly expensive!
3-5-2 Akasaka, Minato-ku;
tel. +81 3 3505 5052
www.takazawa-y.co.jp/en

* **Nicolai Bergmann:** A small establishment, part florist and part restaurant, with excellent little sandwiches. It's in Omotesando, just behind the Prada Tower.
5 Chome-72 Minamiaoyama, Minato-ku; tel. +81 3 5464 0717
www.nicolaibergmann.com

* **Restaurant Bulgari:** An excellent Italian restaurant in a hip neighborhood. A good choice for dinner, as you can admire the lights of the city.
Ginza Tower, 2-7-12 Ginza, Chuo-ku;
tel. +81 3 6362 0555
www.bulgarihotels.com

* **Cicada:** A wonderful place for Mediterranean cuisine in a modern setting. Has a lovely courtyard terrace.
5-7-28 Minami-Aoyama, Minato-ku;
tel. +81 3 6434 1255
www.tysons.jp/cicada

* **Au Gamin de Tokyo:** A place to see (the cooking is performed live) and to be seen (by the local fauna), famous for its truffle omelet!

5-5-10 Shirokane, 2 Fields, Minato-ku;
tel. +81 3 3444 4991
www.gamin2008.com

* **Tera:** Near the Hiroo station, an excellent teppanyaki restaurant with ultra-fresh organic foods!
4-6-7 Nishiazabu Minato-ku;
tel. +81 3 3797 4977

* **Kyubey:** In Ginza, probably the most famous sushi restaurant in Japan—and that's saying something!
7-6, Ginza 8-chome, Chuo-ku;
tel. +81 3 3221 4114
www.kyubey.jp/en

MY STORES

* **Sanrio:** The flagship store where the entire Hello Kitty universe can be found. Perfect for browsing for silly things and bringing back presents.
1st Floor, 2nd Floor, Nishi Ginza;
Department Store, 4-1 Saki, Ginza-ku;
www.sanrio.co.jp/english/store/sh1703100

* **Don Quijote:** A Japanese chain that offers a little of everything: groceries, electronics, clothes. Several stores in Tokyo.
Find retail locations at
www.donki.com/en

* **Takahashi Hiroko:** A contemporary artist who makes magnificent geometric kimonos. His new workshop has a space on the ground floor for exhibits and a shop.
1st Floor, 4-11-2 Narihara, Sumida-ku;
tel. +81 3 6456 1624
www.takahashihiroko.com

* **Mic*Itaya:** An artist who creates magnificent light fixtures out of bamboo and rice paper, using traditional techniques for Japanese lanterns.
4-4118 Kamimeguro, Mehuro-ku;
tel. +81 3 3712 8521
www.micitaya.com

* **Drill Design Inc.:** A studio where the designers work in wood and paper in a very spare, modern style.
2-15-10, Mita, Meguro-ku;
tel. +81 3 3792 6950
www.drill-design.com

* **Wise Wise Tools:** A Japanese brand of household furnishings (furniture, lights, accessories) stripped to their essence—handsome, pure, low-key.
Tokyo Midtown, Galleria/3F/13,
9-7-4 Akasaka Minato-ku
www.wisewise.com

* **Time & Style:** Modern designer style in a Japanese version, with furniture, tableware, and fabrics in a very Zen atmosphere.
Tokyo Midtown, Galleria 3F,
9-7-4 Akasaka Minato-ku;
tel. +81 3 5413 3501
www.timeandstyle.com/en

* **Dover Street Market Ginza, Comme des Garçons:** For hard-core devotees!
6-9-5, Ginza, Chuo-ku;
tel. +81 3 6228 5080
ginza.doverstreetmarket.com

MY OUTINGS

* **The Ghibli Museum:** In the Tokyo suburb of Mitaka, a museum devoted to the most famous animation studio in Japan.
1-1-83 Simorenjaku, Mitaka-ku;
tel. +81 570 055 777
www.ghibli-museum.jp/en

* **Womb:** A nightclub with great ambience. Good spot for a night out.
150-0044 Tokyo, Shibuya-ku;
tel. +81 3 5459 0039
www.womb.co.jp

* **Akihabara:** The electronics district, which is busy night and day.
e-akihabara.jp/e

* Other interesting neighborhoods where I like to walk: Omotesando, Shibuya, Harajuku, Aoyama . . .

MY PARIS RESTAURANTS

MONTMARTRE

✴ Le Coq Rico
93 rue Lepic, 75018 Paris;
tel. +33 01 42 59 82 89
en.lecoqrico.com

✴ Brasserie Barbès
124 boulevard de La Chapelle, 75018
Paris; tel. +33 01 72 01 45 48
www.brasseriebarbes.com

✴ L'Hôtel Particulier
Pavillon D, 23 avenue Junot, 75018
Paris; tel. +33 01 53 41 81 40
hotel-particulier-montmartre.com

PIGALLE

✴ Hôtel Amour
8 rue Navarin, 75018 Paris;
tel. +33 01 48 78 31 80
www.hotelamourparis.fr/en
/restaurant-en

TUILERIES

✴ Hôtel Costes
239-241 rue Saint-Honoré, 75001
Paris; tel. +33 01 42 44 50 00
hotelcostes.com/#/en/costes/22
/restaurant-bar/23/restaurant-terrace

✴ Ferdi
32 rue du Mont-Thabor, 75001 Paris;
tel. +33 01 42 60 82 52

✴ Jin
6 rue de la Sourdière, 75001 Paris;
tel. +33 01 42 61 60 71

✴ Le Café Marly
93 rue de Rivoli, 75001 Paris;
tel. +33 01 49 26 06 60
cafe-marly.com/en

✴ La Belle Époque
36 rue des Petits-Champs, 75002
Paris; tel. +33 01 44 70 05 42

SAINT-GERMAIN

✴ Le Montana
28 rue Saint-Benoît, 75006 Paris;
tel. +33 01 44 39 71 29
www.hotel-lemontana.com/en

✴ Chez Castel
15 rue Princesse, 75006 Paris;
tel. +33 01 40 51 52 80

✴ L'Atelier de Joël Robuchon
5 rue de Montalembert, 75007 Paris;
tel. +33 01 42 22 56 56
atelier-robuchon-saint-germain.com
/en/accueil.php

FLEA MARKET

✴ Ma Cocotte
106 rue des Rosiers, 93400 Saint-
Ouen; tel. +33 01 49 51 70 00
www.macocotte-lespuces.com

BATIGNOLLES

✴ Gare au Gorille
68 rue des Dames, 75017 Paris;
tel. +33 01 42 94 24 02

ÉTOILE

✴ Victoria 1836
12 rue de Presbourg, 75016 Paris;
tel. +33 01 44 17 97 72
www.victoria-1836.com

✴ Pierre Gagnaire
6 rue Balzac, 75008 Paris;
tel. +33 01 58 36 12 50
www.pierre-gagnaire.com/en#

7TH ARRONDISSEMENT

✴ Thoumieux
79 rue Saint-Dominique, 75007 Paris;
tel. +33 01 47 05 49 75
www.thoumieux.fr/en

✴ Rosa Bonheur
Quai d'Orsay, Port des Invalides,
75007 Paris; tel. +33 01 47 53 66 92
www.rosabonheur.fr/english-digest

15TH ARRONDISSEMENT

✴ Eclectic
2 rue Linois, 75015 Paris;
tel. +33 01 77 36 70 00
www.restauranteclectic.fr

✴ Mazeh
65 rue des Entrepreneurs, 75015
Paris; tel. +33 01 45 75 33 89
www.mazeh.com

LES HALLES

✴ Les Bains
7 rue du Bourg l'Abbé, 75003 Paris;
tel. +33 01 42 77 07 07
www.lesbains-paris.com/en/dining

11TH ARRONDISSEMENT

✴ Ober Mamma
107 boulevard Richard Lenoir, 75011
Paris; tel. +33 01 58 30 62 78
www.bigmammagroup.com
/ober-mamma

✴ Septime
80 rue de Charonne, 75011 Paris;
tel. +33 01 43 67 38 29
www.septime-charonne.fr

✴ Unico
15 rue Paul Bert, 75011 Paris;
tel. +33 01 43 67 68 08
www.resto-unico.com/accueil

BAGNOLET

✴ Mama Shelter
109 rue de Bagnolet, 75020 Paris;
tel. +33 01 43 48 48 48
www.mamashelter.com/en/paris
/restaurants/restaurant

ALÉSIA

✴ Le Severo
8 rue des Plantes, 75014 Paris;
tel. +33 01 45 40 40 91

MY ADDRESSES IN FRANCE, OUTSIDE OF PARIS

HOME DECORATION

✶ Cink
2 rue Paul Bert,
13080 Aix-en-Provence
www.cinkhome.com

✶ Cour Intérieure
44 rue Luis-Mariano and 9 avenue
Victor-Hugo, 65200 Biarritz
www.cour-interieure.fr

✶ Atelier 29
14 cours de Verdun, 33300 Bordeaux;
tel. +33 05 56 38 81 05

✶ Jane de Boy
32/34 boulevard de la Plage, 33950
Lège-Cap-Ferret
www.janedeboy.com

✶ Suite 13
13 rue du Maréchal-Leclerc, 35800
Dinard

✶ Maison HAND
11 bis rue Jarente, 69000 Lyon
www.maison-hand.com

✶ L'Âne Bleu
62 rue Breteuil, 13000 Marseille
www.anebleu.com

✶ Violette
2 rue du Petit-Saint-Jean,
34000 Montpellier
www.boutique-violette.fr

✶ La Villa 1901
63 avenue du Général-Leclerc,
54100 Nancy
www.lavilla1901.fr/en

✶ La Cachette d'Ali Babette
37 rue de Gigant, 44000 Nantes
www.lacachettedalibabette.com

✶ Robinson M.
10 rue Delille, 06100 Nice
www.marierobinson.fr

✶ Via Nomade
2 rue Élie-Fréron, 29000 Quimper
www.vianomade.com

✶ Pièce Unik
30 rue de l'Hôpital, 76100 Rouen;
tel. +33 02 35 98 59 81
www.galerie-pieceunique.com

✶ Libellule
10 rue Jaume-Roux, 13210 Saint-
Rémy-de-Provence
www.libelluledeparis.net

✶ CJ Interiors
12 avenue Foch, place des Lices,
83990 Saint-Tropez

✶ Terra Rosa
3 rue des Prêtres, 31500 Toulouse
www.terrarosa.fr

✶ Des Isles
5 rue du Phare, 83400 Porquerolles
www.desisles.fr

MUSEUMS

* **Musée Pierre Soulages**
Avenue Victor-Hugo, 12000 Rodez; tel.
+33 05 65 73 82 60
www.musee-soulages.rodezagglo.fr
/museum-soulages

* **CAPC Musée d'Art
Contemporain de Bordeaux**
7 rue Ferrere, 33300 Bordeaux;
tel. +33 05 56 00 81 50
www.capc-bordeaux.fr/en

* **Les Abattoirs**
76 allée Charles-de-Fitte, 31500
Toulouse; tel. +33 05 34 51 10 60
www.lesabattoirs.org/en

* **MuCEM**
7 promenade Robert-Laffont, 13000
Marseille
www.mucem.org/en

* **Mémorial de l'Abolition de
l'Esclavage**
Quai de la Fosse, 44000 Nantes
www.memorial.nantes.fr/en

* **Château La Coste**
2750 route de la Cride, 13610
Le Puy-Sainte-Réparade
www.chateau-la-coste.com/en

BARS AND
RESTAURANTS

* **La Cigale**
4 place Graslin, 44000 Nantes
www.lacigale.fr/en

* **La Côte Saint Jacques**
14 faubourg de Paris, 89300 Joigny
www.cotesaintjacques.com/en

* **Les Vapeurs**
160 boulevard Fernand-Moureaux,
14360 Trouville-sur-Mer
www.lesvapeurs.fr/en

* **La Passarelle**
52 rue Plan-Fourmiguier,
13007 Marseille
www.restaurantlapassarelle.fr

* **La Co(o)rniche**
46 avenue Louis-Gaume,
33115 Pyla-sur-Mer
www.lacoorniche-pyla.com/en

* **La Reine des Prés**
7 avenue de Chavoires,
74940 Annecy-le-Vieux
www.lareinedespres.fr/en

* **L'Arnsbourg**
18 Untermuhlthal,
57230 Baerenthal
www.arnsbourg.com/fr

* **Hétéroclito**
Chemin de la Plage, 64210 Guéthary

HOTELS

* **La Ferme Saint Simenon**
20 route Adolphe-Marais,
14600 Honfleur
www.fermestsimon.com

* **Chez Boulan**
2 rue des Palmiers,
33950 Lège-Cap-Ferret
www.huitresboulan.fr/jardin-boulan
-capferret.php

* **La Réserve**
Chemin de la Quessine,
83350 Ramatuelle
www.lareserve-ramatuelle.com/en

* **L'Hôtel Particulier**
4 rue de la Monnaie, 13200 Arles
www.hotel-particulier.com/v2/en

Thanks to...

Yasmine, Roman, Milo, and Marc, my family, my friends, my loves.

Édouard, Fanny, and Béatrice, without whom I could never
have given this book its handcrafted look, which means
so much to me—and still have delivered it on time!
Florent and the whole Studio crew, for their help and advice.

All the photographers and illustrators who have given this book its
visuals: Agence Louis Benech, Francis Amiand, Christophe Bielsa,
Delphine Cauly, Michel Figuet, Nicolas Grandmaison, Sylvie Lancrenon,
Guillaume de Laubier, Luna, Nicolas Matheus, Vincent Perez,
Franco Tettamanti/Licencity, Alexis Tourreau, Tung Walsh.

All the experts who contributed their words to this
book, making it shine with their talent.

Véronique, Danièle, Yaël, Delphine, and, of course,
Sophie and Alexandrine, who were with me every day
while this book was being written and produced.

And finally all those who have inspired me, encouraged
me, trusted me since the start of my adventure in
the fascinating, crazy world of interior design.

CAPTIONS

pp. 12–13 Plate: Sicilia by Maison Sarah Lavoine. Mortar: Tom Dixon. Lamp: vintage.

p. 14 Mirror: Ovo, by Maison Sarah Lavoine. Coffee table: Tokyo, by Maison Sarah Lavoine.

p. 15 Coffee table: Yves Klein. Red pot: Jean-Pierre Raynaud.

pp. 16–17 Coffee table: Roger Capron. Sofa: Noa, by Maison Sarah Lavoine. Mirrors: Ovo and Organique, by Maison Sarah Lavoine.

pp. 18–19 Selection of vintage furniture by Galerie Hervouet. Sofa: Box, by Maison Sarah Lavoine.

p. 20 Lantern: Paola Navone.

p. 22 Furniture: Galerie Jacques Hervouet.

p. 24 Wall light: Vadim, by Maison Sarah Lavoine. Hanging lamp: Mategot. Spotlights: Ruben.

p. 25 Straw hanging lamp: Gervasoni. Glass hanging lamp: Gilles Oudin. Pole lamp: Florence Lopez. Gun Lamp by Starck.

p. 26 Galerie Hervouet.

p. 27 Lamp: Vintage.

p. 28 Candleholders: Serax. Sofa: Yasmine by Maison Sarah Lavoine. Lamp: Florence Lopez.

pp. 30–31 Candles: Saint Roch, Saint Honoré, Bac, Nyx, Gaïa, Eos, by Maison Sarah Lavoine, Stone Paris.

p. 33 Chair: Campanino.

p. 34 Sculpture: Nathalie Decoster. Photo: Galerie M Bart.

p. 35 Hanging lamp: Vertigo, by Constance Guisset for Petite Friture. Sofa: Milo, by Maison Sarah Lavoine. Photo: Galerie Acte 2.

pp. 40–41 Mirrors: Ovo and Organique, by Maison Sarah Lavoine. Ceramic wall sculpture: Sarah Lavoine. Polaroids: Marc Lavoine.

pp. 42–43 Mirror: Hubert le Gall. Hanging lamp: Mategot. Polaroids: Marc Lavoine. Lamp: Florence Lopez. Chair: Charlotte Perriand.

pp. 54–55 Plates: Sicilia. Cup and saucer: Aboro, by Bernardaud.

p. 56 Table: Tolix.

pp. 58–59 Kitchen: Boffi.

pp. 60–61 Kitchen: Boffi. Dishes: Aboro, by Bernardaud.

p. 65 Bench: Le Tube, by Maison Sarah Lavoine. Table: Sam, by Maison Sarah Lavoine.

p. 71 Dishes: Sicilia, by Maison Sarah Lavoine.

p. 76 Lamps: Michel Klein. Bench: ALM. Sculpture: Nathalie Decoster. Pearls on the wall: Julie Cheng. Drawings: Katrin Bremermann. Hanging lamp: Gilles Oudin.

p. 78 Swing lamp: Jean Prouvé.

p. 83 Paintings: MB Art LA.

p. 86 Painting: Vintage. Lamp: Azucena.

p. 90 Bed linen: Chez Zoé. Pillows and bedspread: Caravane.

p. 93 Drawings: Fabrice Hyber.

p. 94 Tree wall art: Zoé Ouvrier. Wall lamp: Gras. Armchairs: secondhand at Florence Lopez.

p. 96 Lamp: Azucena. Nightstand: JNL. Object: James Hayon for Baccarat. Art: Peter Beard, Galerie Kamel Mennour.

pp. 106–7 Candle: Bougie XL, by Bonpoint. Pocket-sized perfume: Atelier Cologne. Ring: Sarah, by Stone Paris.

p. 109 Bathrobe: Atelier Zoé.

p. 114 Nail polish: Sarah Lavoine, for My Little Box.

p. 126 Leather jacket: Balenciaga.

p. 127 Hat: Maison Michel. Sneakers: Stan Smith, by Adidas.

p. 129 Shoes: Gianvito Rossi. Jewels: Stone Paris.

p. 140 Mirrors: Mini-Me, by Maison Sarah Lavoine.

p. 143 Bunk bed: Perludi.

p. 156 Straw bag: Pampelonne, by Maison Sarah Lavoine.

p. 159 Armchair: Acapulco.

p. 166 Table linen: Merci.

p. 167 Tablecloths: Csao.

CREDITS

© Illustration Sarah Lavoine: pp. 12–13, 16–17, 21, 24 right, 27, 30–31, 39, 46, 48, 49, 50, 54–55, 57 bottom, 63 bottom, 68, 69, 73, 74, 79 left, 94 bottom, 99 bottom, 106–7, 111, 113, 114, 115, 117, 120 bottom, 121 bottom, 136, 137, 145, 147, 149 right, 163, 164, 165 bottom and right, 168, 169, 174, 176, 186–7.

© Francis Amiand: pp. 14, 18–19, 22, 25 left and top, 26, 29, 33, 34, 35, 52, 56, 57 left and top, 60–61, 62, 71, 76, 84 bottom left and right, 86, 92, 94 top, 96, 97 top, 98 bottom, 100 top, 122 top left and bottom center, 140, 143.

© Yaël Abrot: pp. 20, 24 center, 64, 65, 66, 75, 79 bottom right, 83, 88, 89 top, 99 top, 112, 116, 124, 126, 127, 128, 129,

130 bottom, 131 center, 133, 134, 144, 146, 149 top, 156, 158, 166, 167, 170–1, 172, 173, 175.

© Christophe Bielsa: p. 110.

© Delphine Cauly: p. 28.

© Michel Figuet: pp. 15, 25 bottom.

© Nicolas Grandmaison: pp. 25 center, 42, 43, 44, 57 bottom, 79 center right, 81 top, 84 top, 85, 89 bottom, 90, 93, 94 center, 97 left, 101 top, 103, 122 bottom right and top right, 151 top, 159.

© Sylvie Lancrenon: pp. 5, 130 top.

© Guillaume de Laubier for *Sarah Lavoine*, Éditions de la Martinière, 2010:

pp. 58–59, 63, 70, 78, 79 top right, 80, 81 bottom, 82, 91 top, 95, 97 center, 98 top, 100 bottom, 101 right, 108, 109, 118, 121 top, 122 top center, 135, 142, 150, 151 bottom, 165 top left.

© Agence Louis Benech: pp. 160, 162.

© Luna: p. 155.

© Nicolas Matheus: pp. 24 left, 91, 104, 119, 122 bottom left.

© Vincent Perez: p. 153.

© Franco Tettamanti/Licencity: pp. 10, 51.

© Alexis Toureau: pp. 45, 99 center, 120 top.

© Tung Walsh: p. 131 bottom.

A leading interior designer,

SARAH LAVOINE,

her agency, and her boutiques have become
synonymous with Parisian taste, contemporary
aesthetics, and craftsmanship. Her line of
home goods is available at Barney's New York, and
her work has been featured in the *New York Times*,
the *Wall Street Journal*, *Vogue*, and more.